CANYON COUNTRY KIDDIES

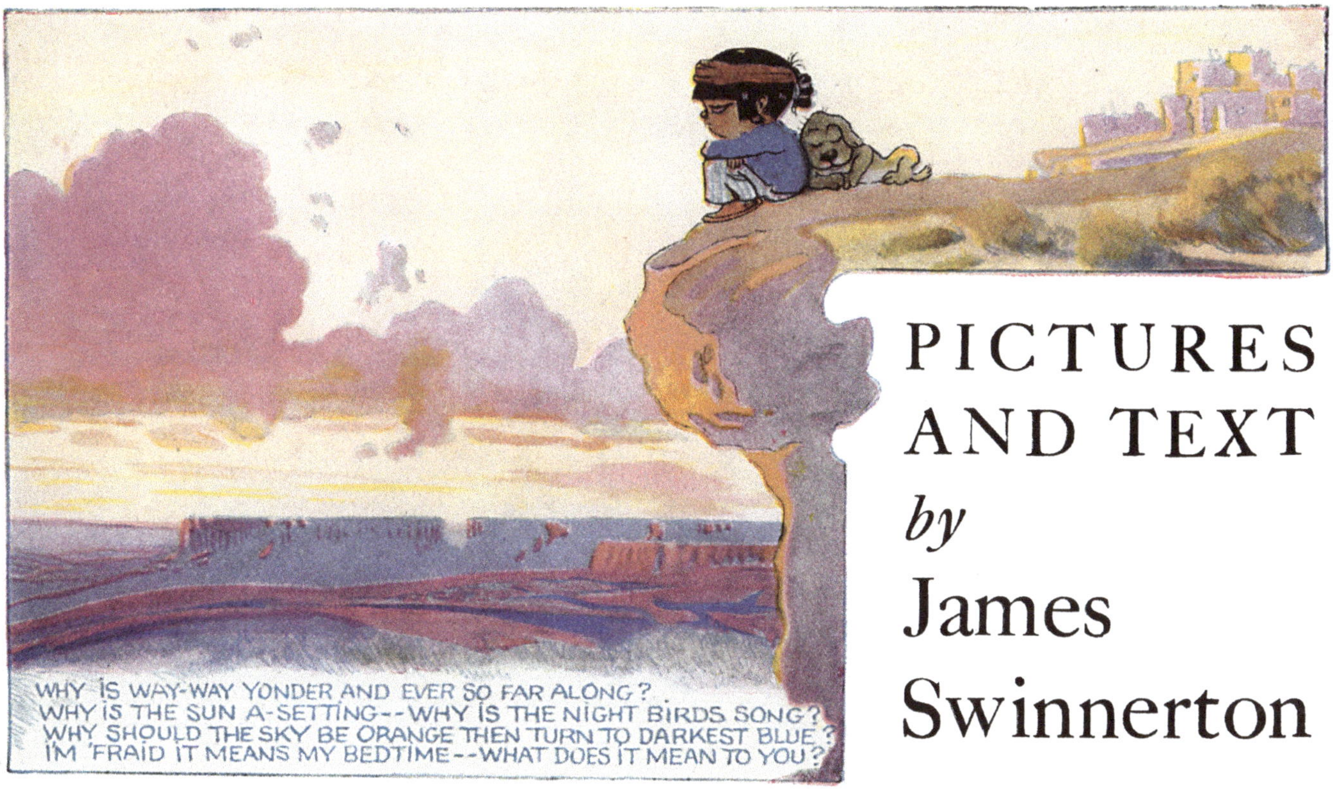

WHY IS WAY-WAY YONDER AND EVER SO FAR ALONG?
WHY IS THE SUN A-SETTING--WHY IS THE NIGHT BIRDS SONG?
WHY SHOULD THE SKY BE ORANGE THEN TURN TO DARKEST BLUE?
I'M 'FRAID IT MEANS MY BEDTIME--WHAT DOES IT MEAN TO YOU?

PICTURES AND TEXT
by
James Swinnerton

TO MY DAUGHTER

MARY ELIZABETH SWINNERTON

Canyon Country Kiddies, by James Swinnerton
First published 1923

CoachwhipBooks.com

ISBN 1-61646-070-9
ISBN-13 978-1-61646-070-9

CANYON COUNTRY KIDDIES

Tewa is calling to hear the echo
answer him,
And from where he stands by the
monster cavern's rim
Calling out so loudly, and echo
answering low,
Some prehistoric kiddie called
ten thousand years ago.

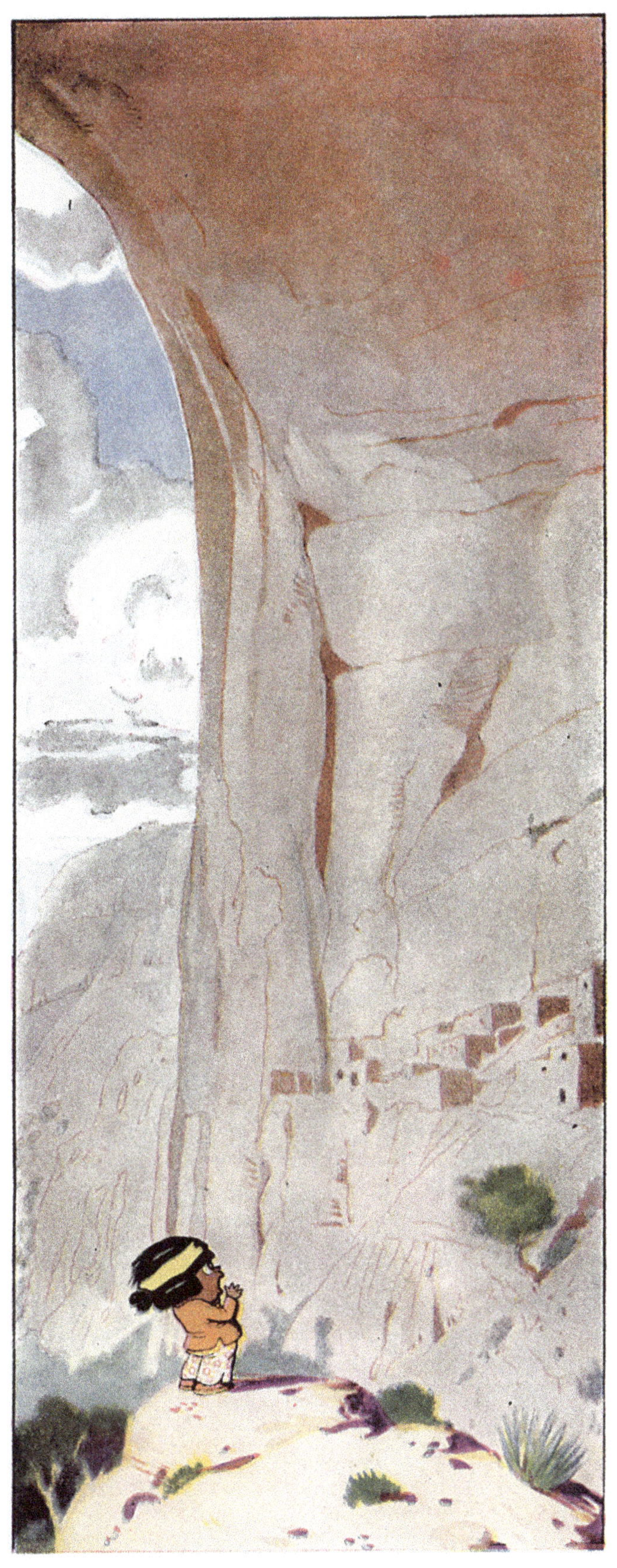

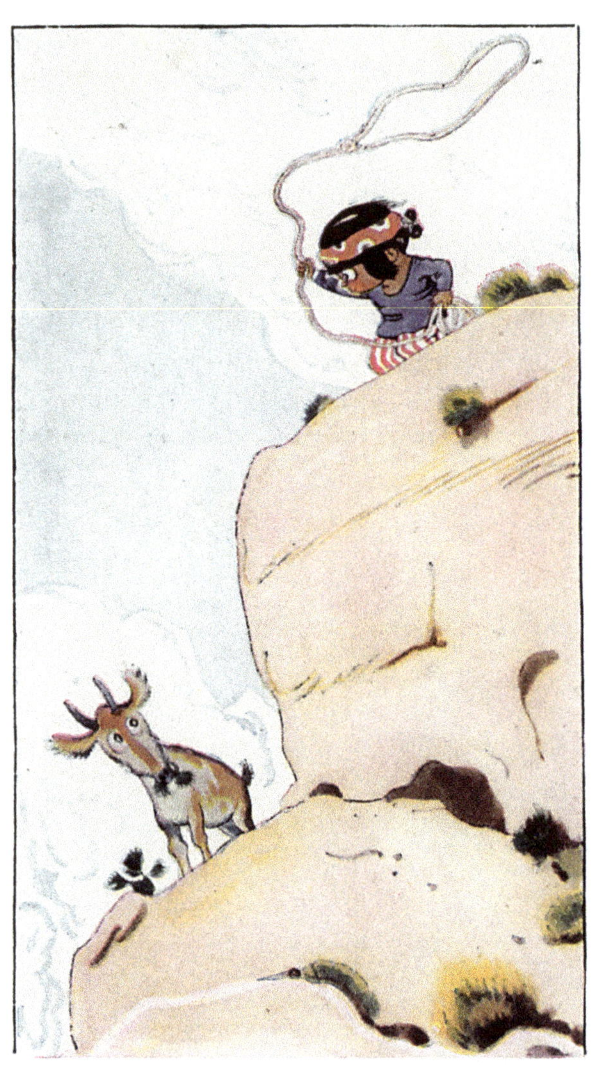

This little boy with his trusty rope
Hopes to lasso the Antelope,
But the Antelope doesn't seem to fear
Any danger by being near;
'Cause in a jiffy, maybe not that,
He could be a mile from where he's
at.

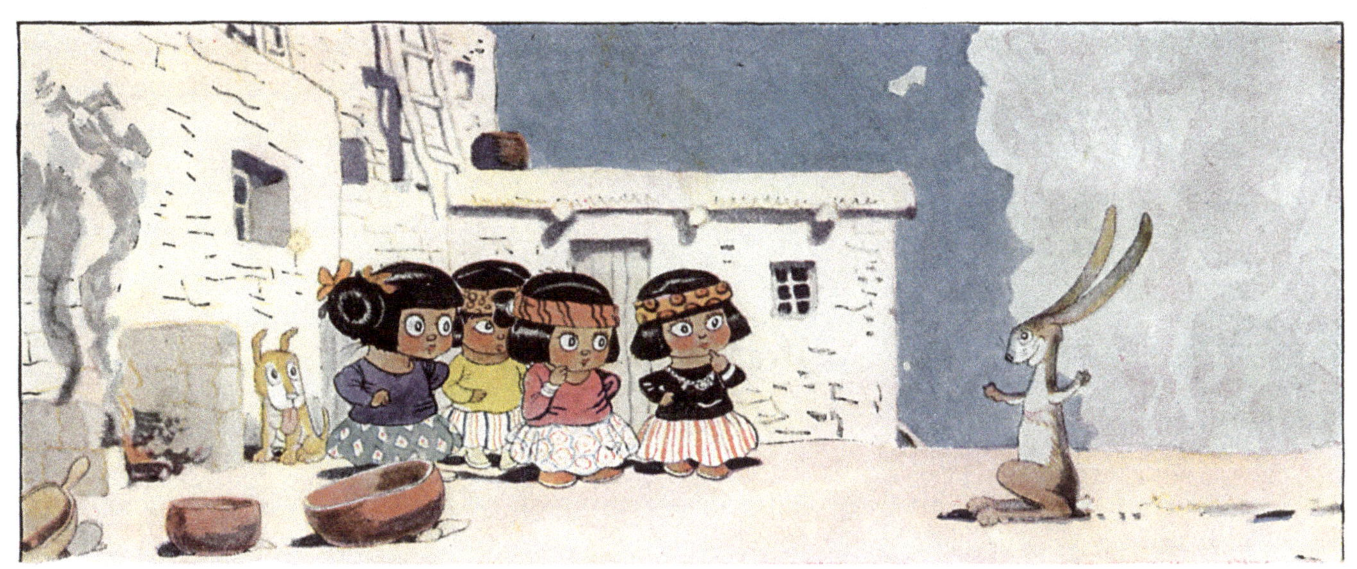

Said the cooks, "Shall we broil him
or boil him
Or roast him or fry him all brown?"
And, worrying lest they should
spoil him,
They puckered their heads in a
frown.

"Since I'm causin' you all of this
trouble"
(And he wiggled his whiskers in
glee)
"I'll not mind at all if you double
Some other Jack Rabbit for me."

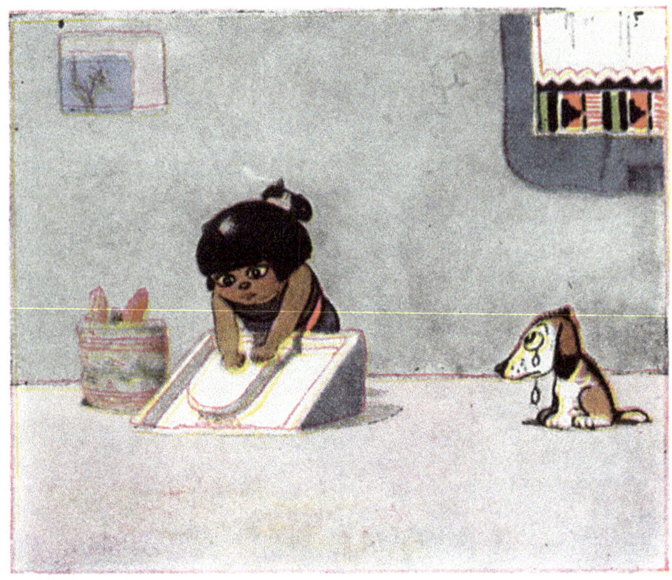

Te-ka works at grinding corn,
Her doggie's name is Ben-nay.
He's looking on with eye forlorn,
'Cause he can't help her any.

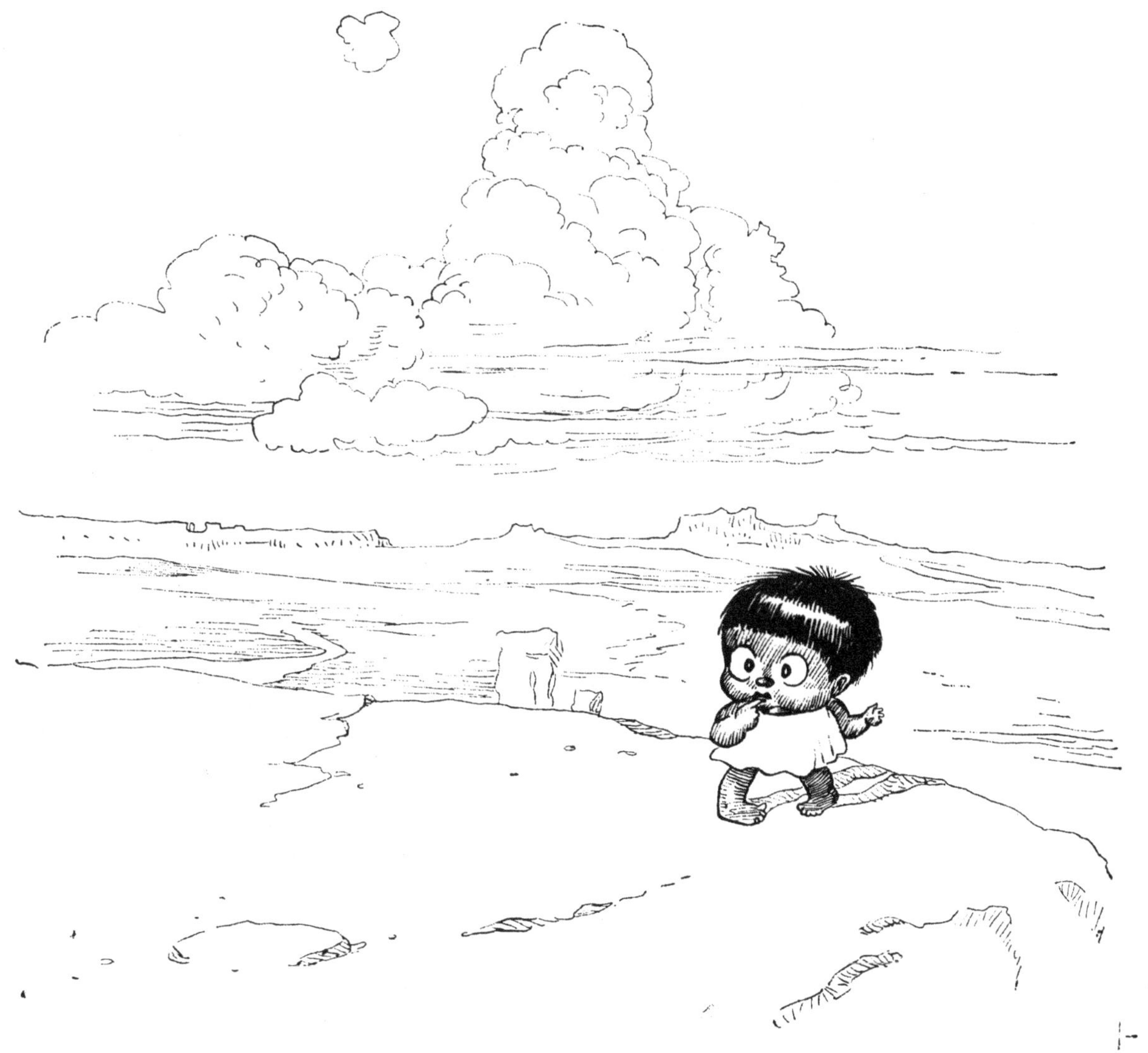

Here's Te-ka's brother worrying his silly little head
As to when the corn she's grinding will be cooked up into
bread.

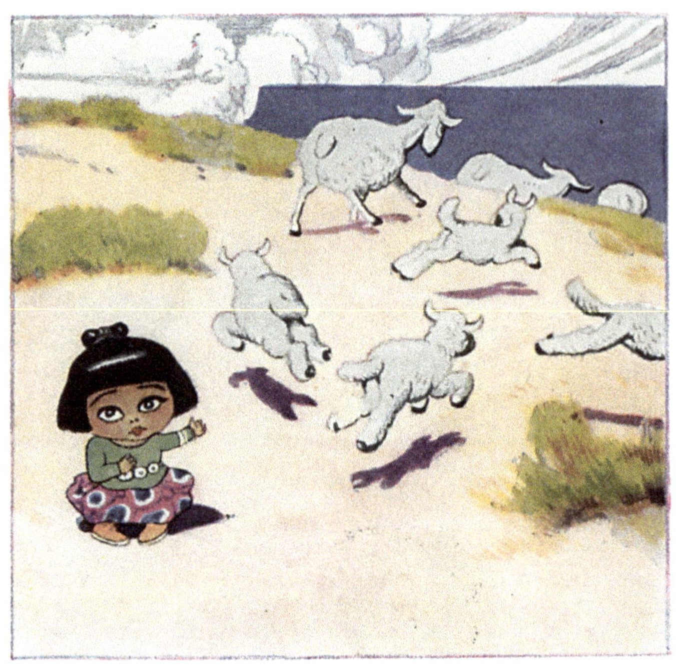

I've often heard of the lamb that fol-
lowed Mary
To her school, and tales that tell of others.
But my Lambs are different; in fact
they're quite contrary.
They never follow me, but keep on following their mothers.

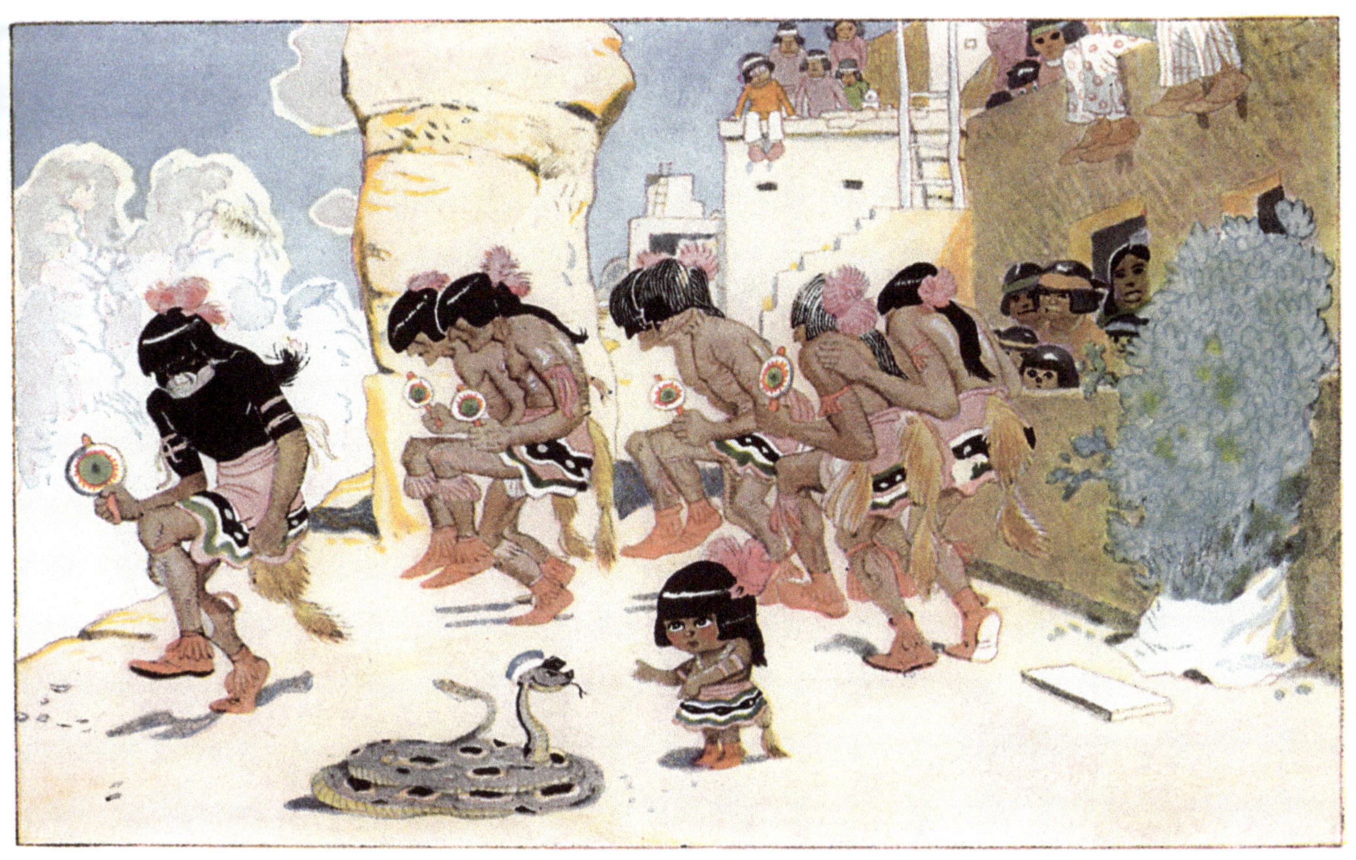

Messenger Snake, go down below
To the roots of things that grow.
Tell them to grow strong and fast,
So the harvest may be past
And the corn be put away
Before the first cold winter's day.

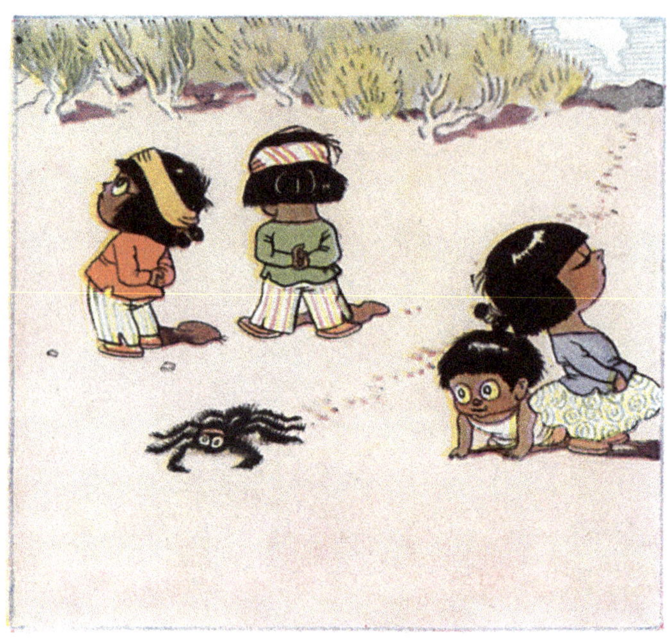

The Tarantula has whiskers very much
overgrown
And he is so lazy he never keeps them
trimmed.
Socially therefore he's left very much
alone.
No one has anything at all to do with him.

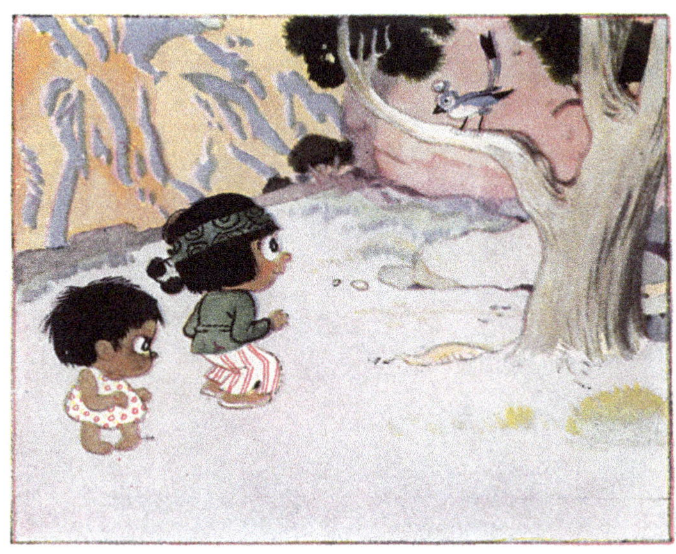

This birdie's called the Chissy-woosh.
He wears a topknot on his head.
And if you find him on a bush
He'll bring you luck, 'tis said.

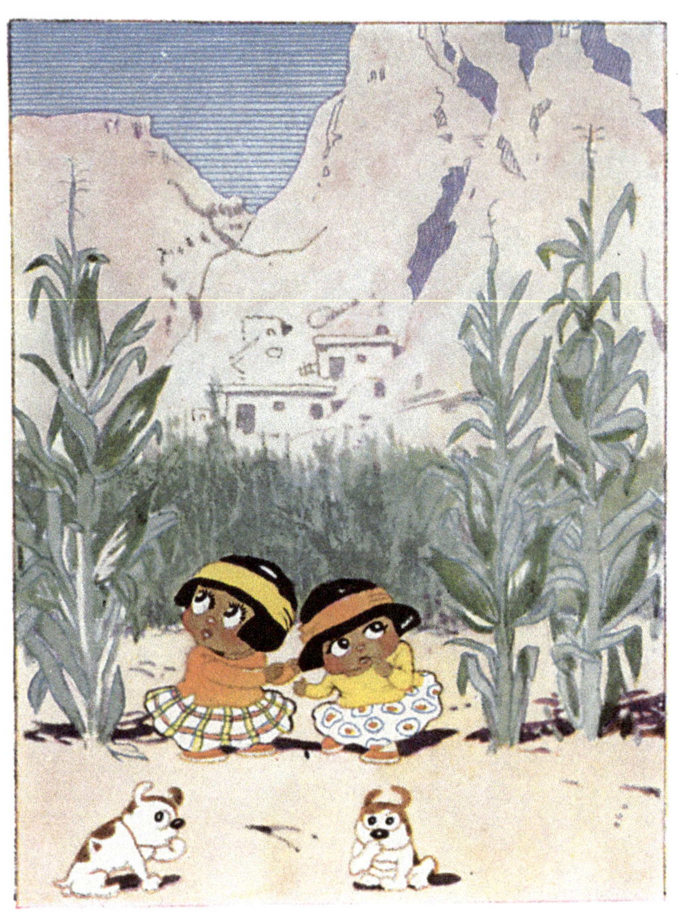

Never tell a secret while in a field
of corn,
All is not as safe as it appears.
Once your secret's out, you'd
surely be forlorn,
'Cause corn, you know, has
many, many ears.

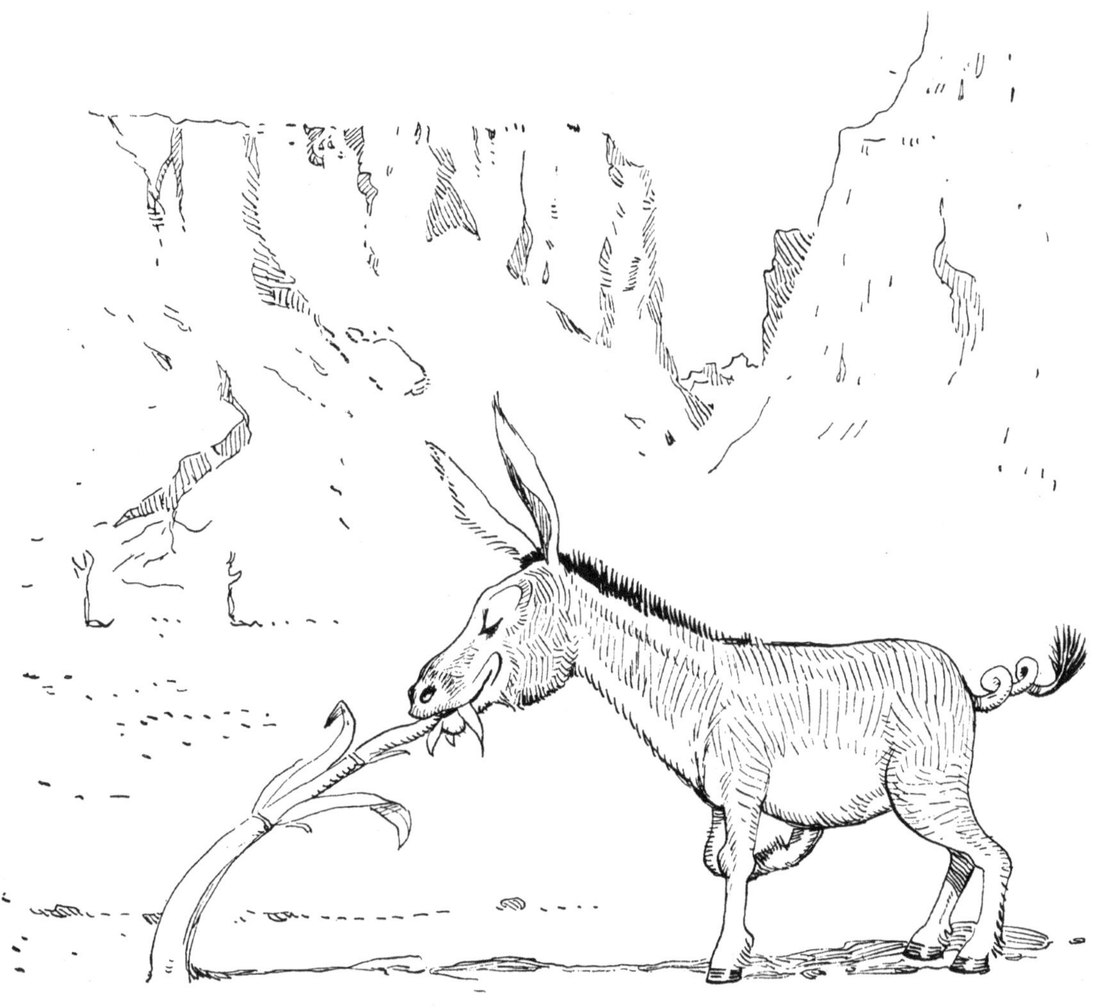

The Burro's eating up the corn and we will all be blest
If he hasn't eaten up the ears together with the rest.

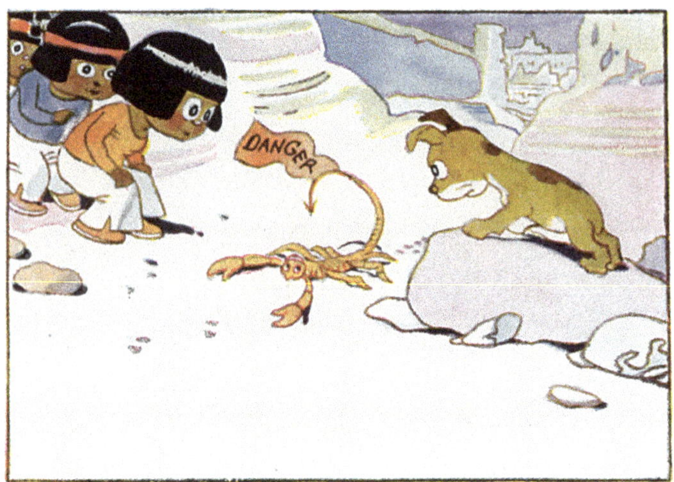

The Scorpion has a spiffley stunt,
As most always without fail
Instead of biting from his front
He will bite you with his tail.

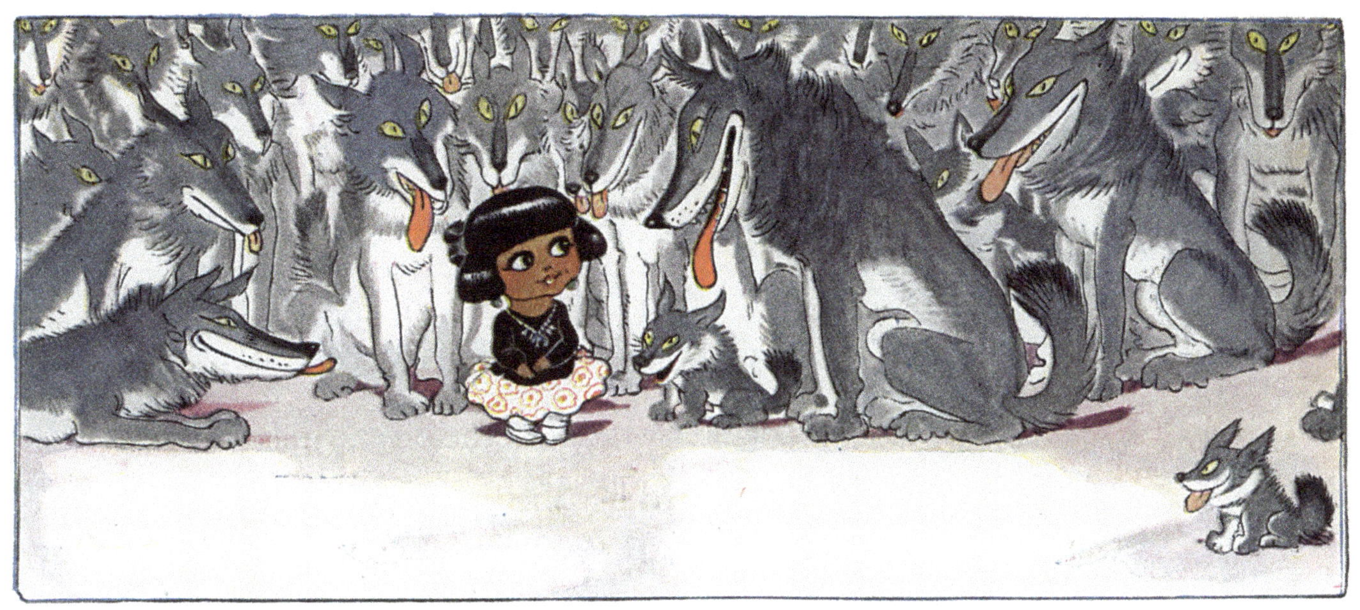

This little Maid
Is not afraid,
Even with wolves to greet her.
She has no charm
To ward off harm,
But still the wolves won't eat her.

They would if they could,
They could if they would—
She's risking a sudden decease;
Not that she's tough—
She just isn't enough
To give them a bite apiece.

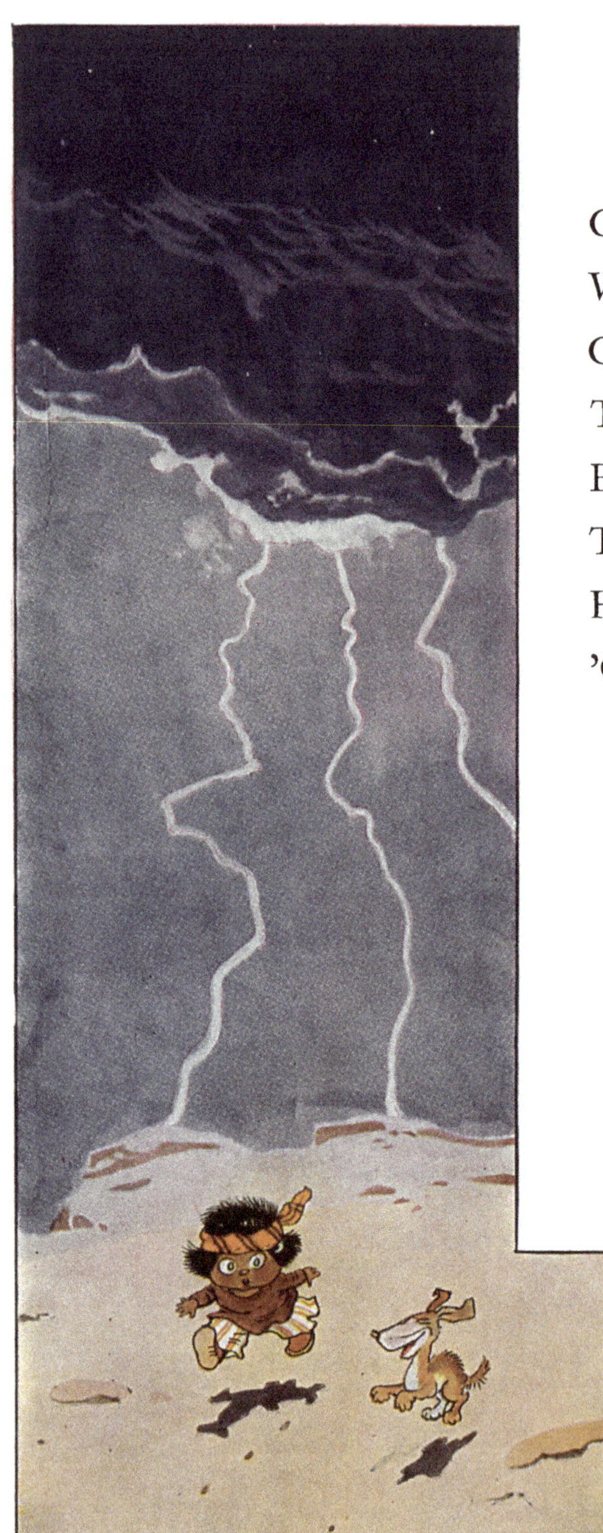

Of course, the little Boy is not afraid
When he hears the thunder bang and roll.
Oh, no, indeed, he's not dismayed.
There is no fear in his little soul.
But the thought to him has just occurred
That to his home on the mesa's rim
He'd best be flying swift as a bird
'Cause his mother might be needing him.

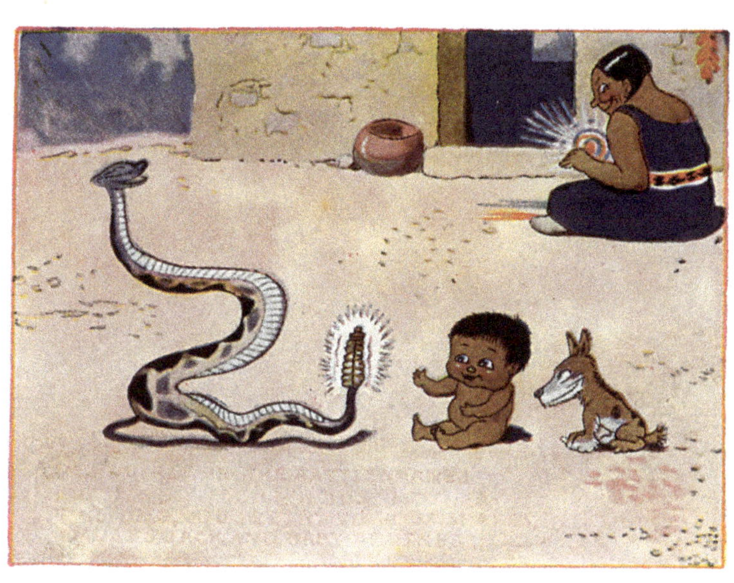

In Hopi-land the Rattlesnakes
Are glad to help a busy mother:
This one, you see, by vig'rous shakes
Amuses Jack and Baby Brother.

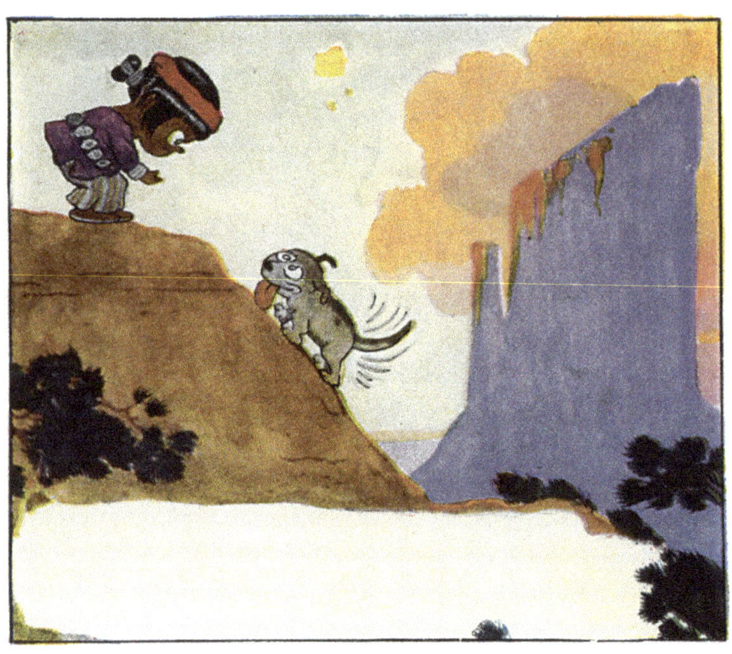

Why does the Doggie strain and pant?
His tongue hangs out and his feet are
draggin'.
Will he reach the top? Oh dear, he can't
'Cause his tail's behind, and that's a wag-
gin'.

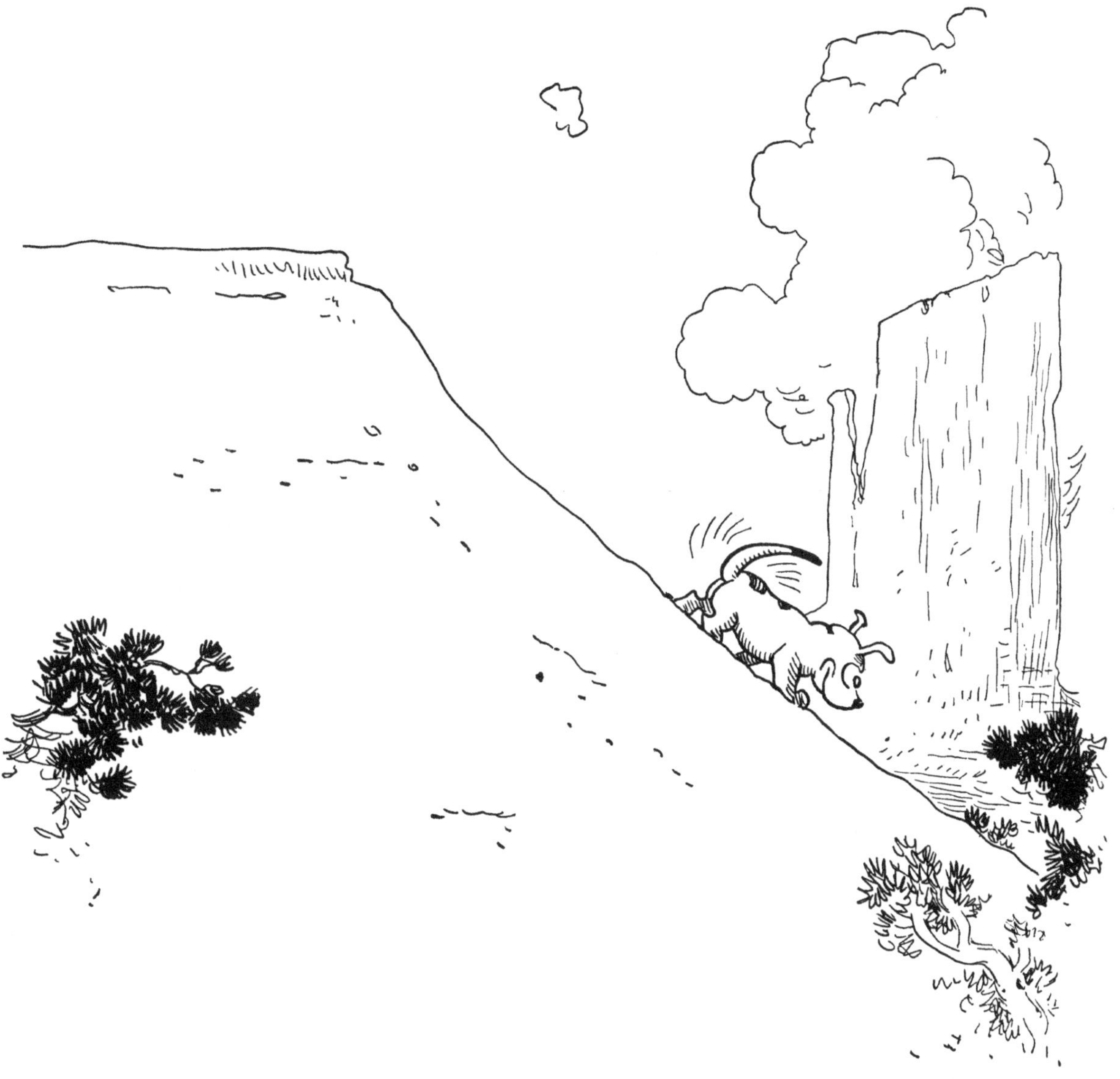

The Doggie went clear to the top and then
He turned right around and went down again.

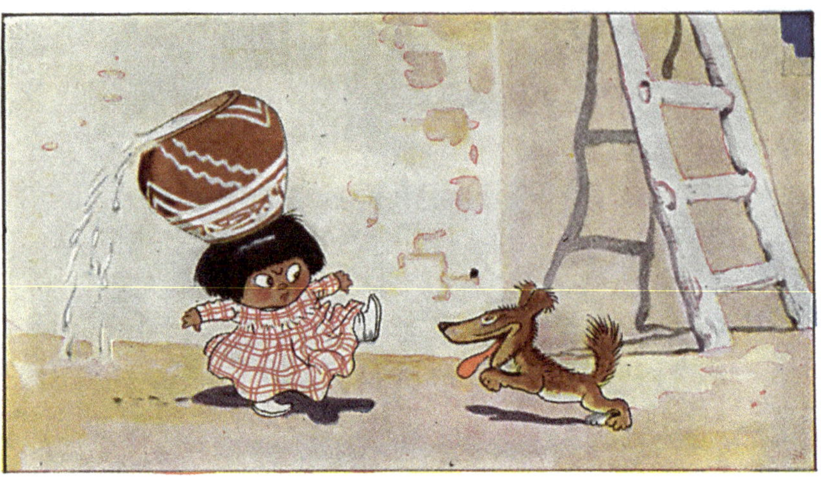

The little Dog is doin' what he knows he
hadn't oughter,
Pesterin' his mistress who's been sent to
bring some water.
And if the water falls, he'd best go far
away,
Or he'll feel very sorry for just about a
day.

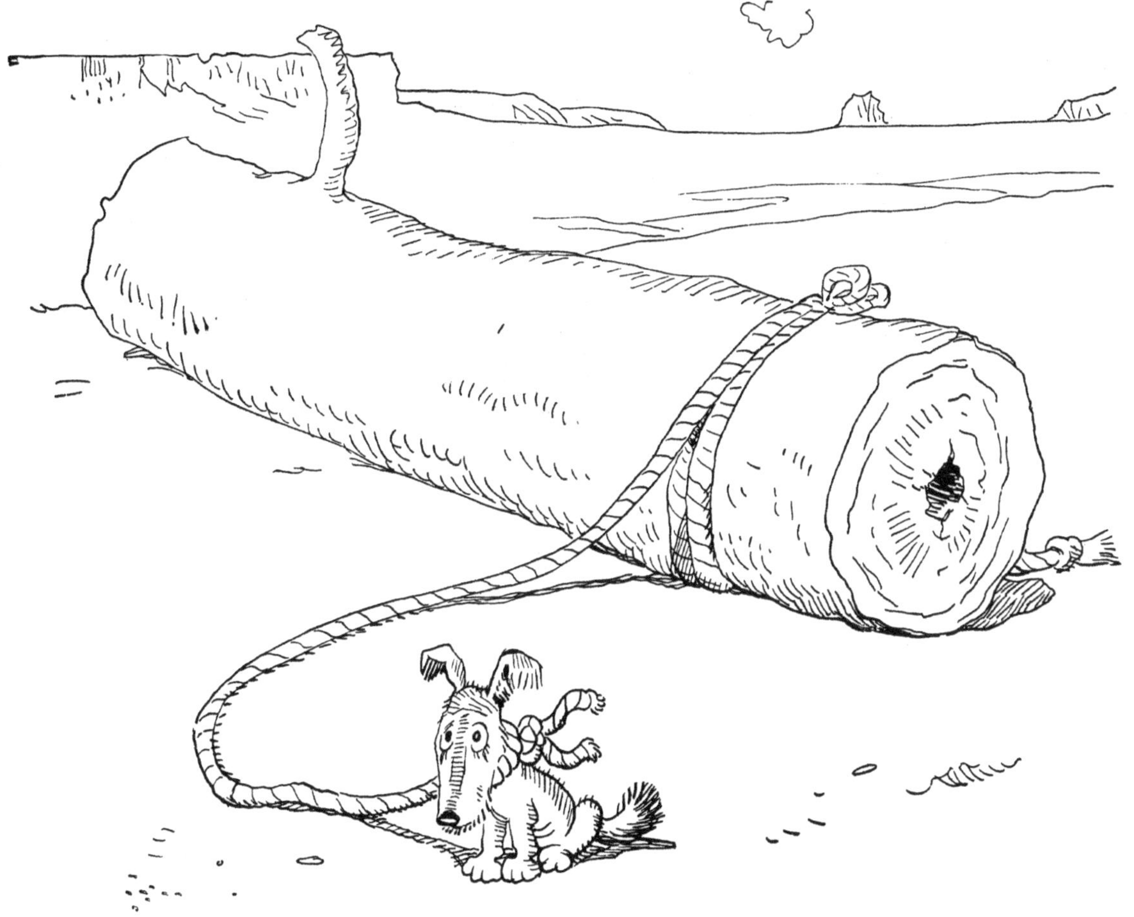

Oh, sad to tell,
The water fell.
Now see the Dog
Stays by a log!

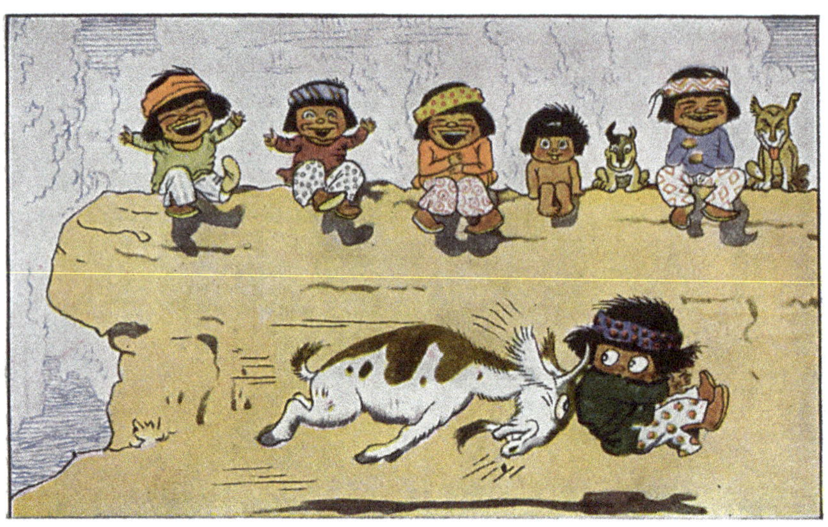

This lady Goat at butting was woefully
adept.
The kids she bumped were sore for days
and days.
Yet they loved her and agreed she was
sweet and lovely 'cept
She was much, oh, much too forward in
her ways.

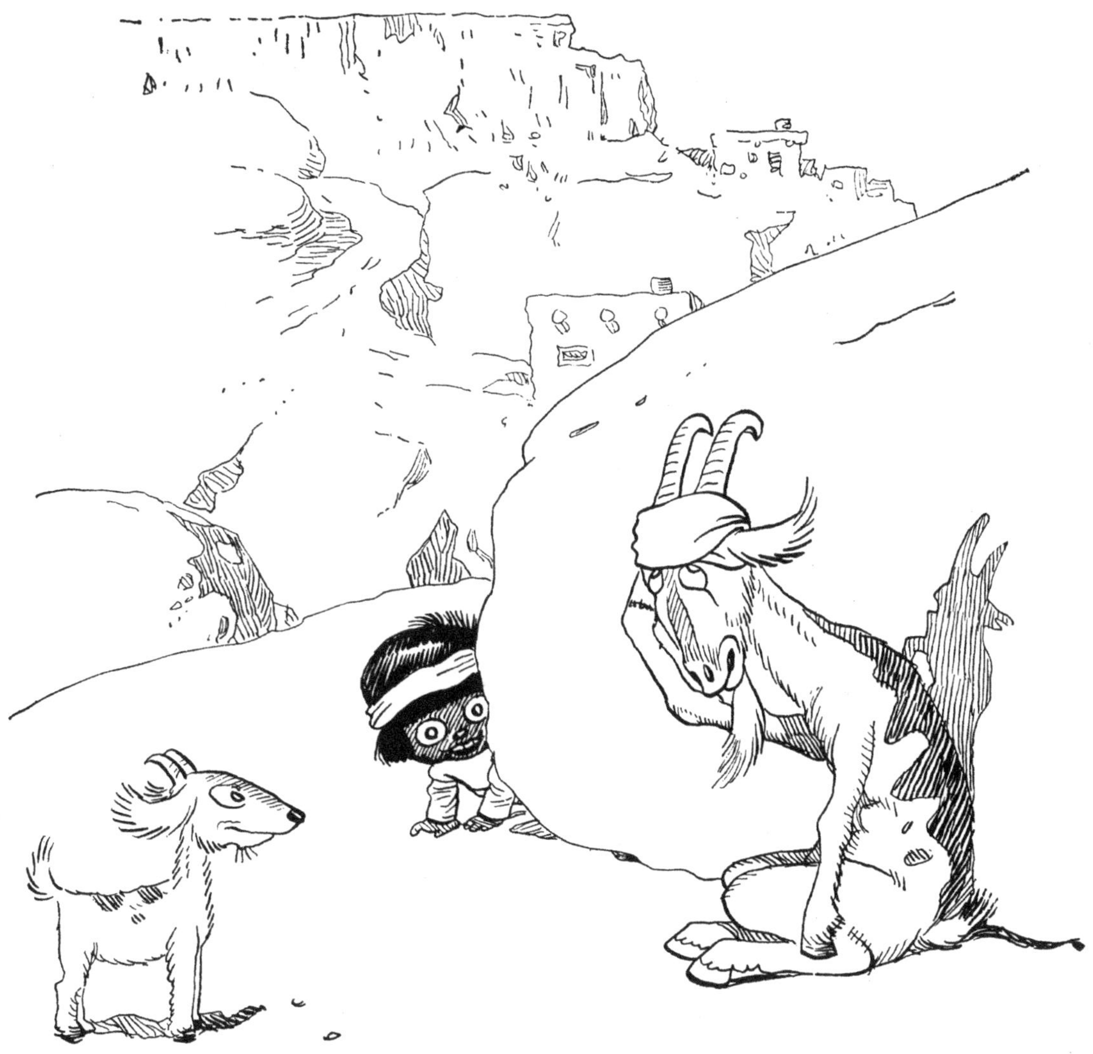

For bumpin' an' for buttin' for bein' harsh and horrid,
This very Goat has justly got a headache in her forehead.

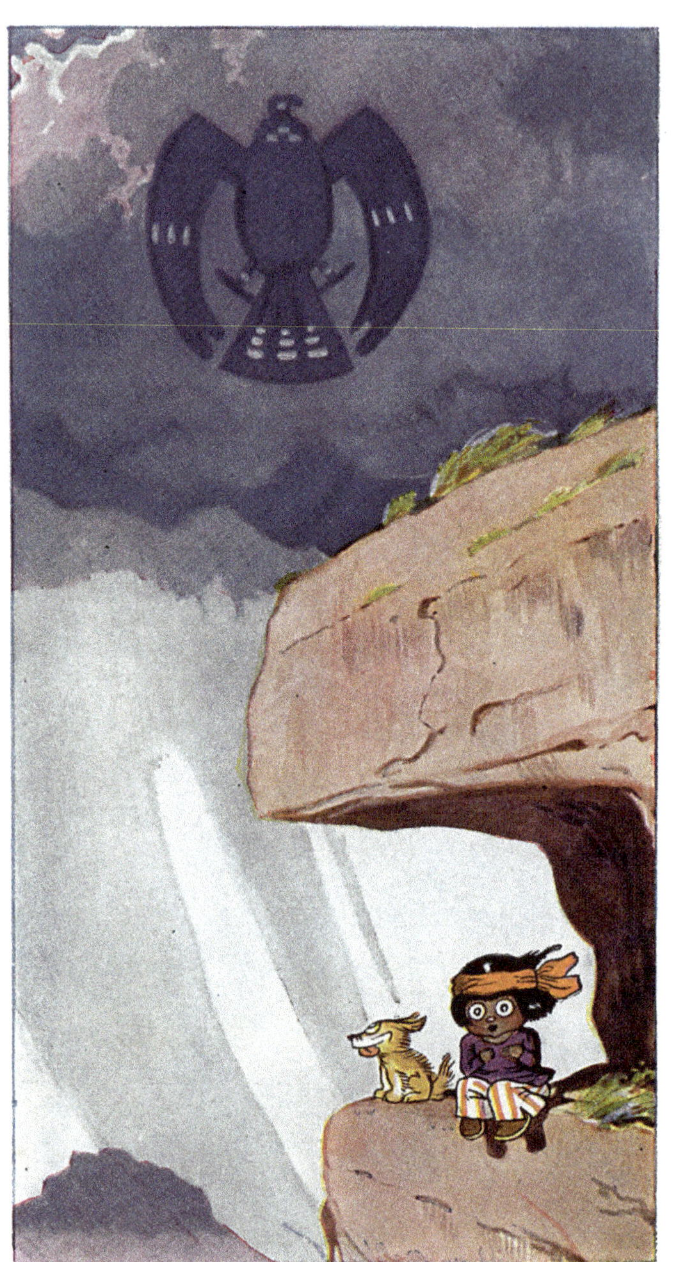

The Thunder Bird is a tough old
bird,
He causes the wind and rain.
Just how he does it I've never
heard,
But he does it just the same.

"I don't think it's right," said little Te-ho-
te,
"That I'm put to bed when the dark comes
along,
When that foolish and noisy little Coy-o-
te,
Can cut up an' ki-yi the whole night long."

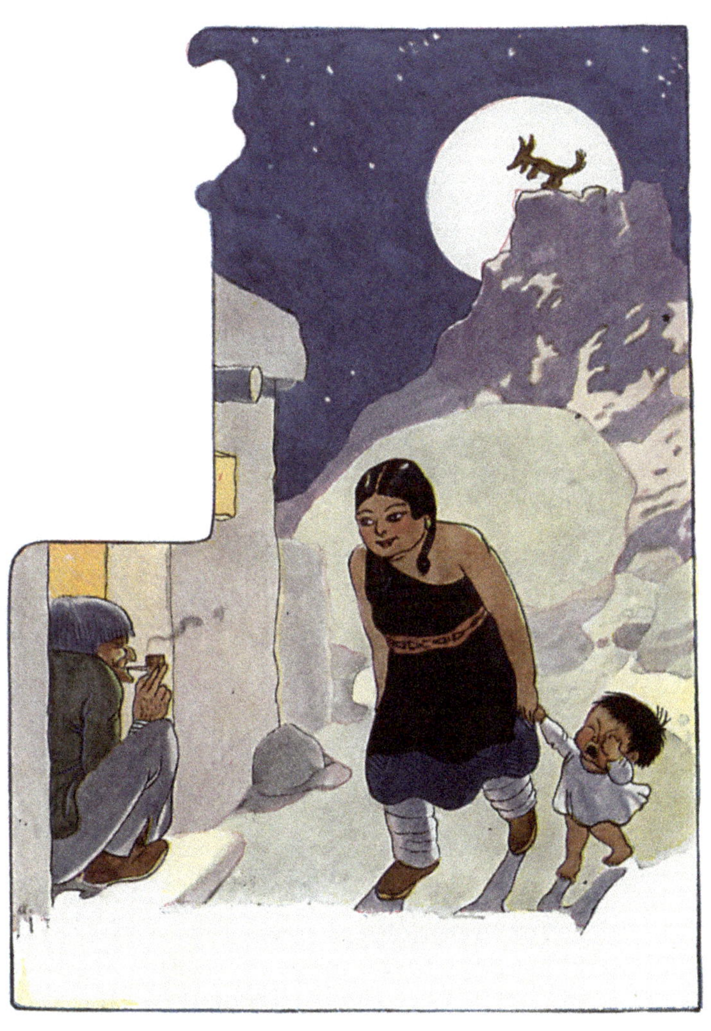

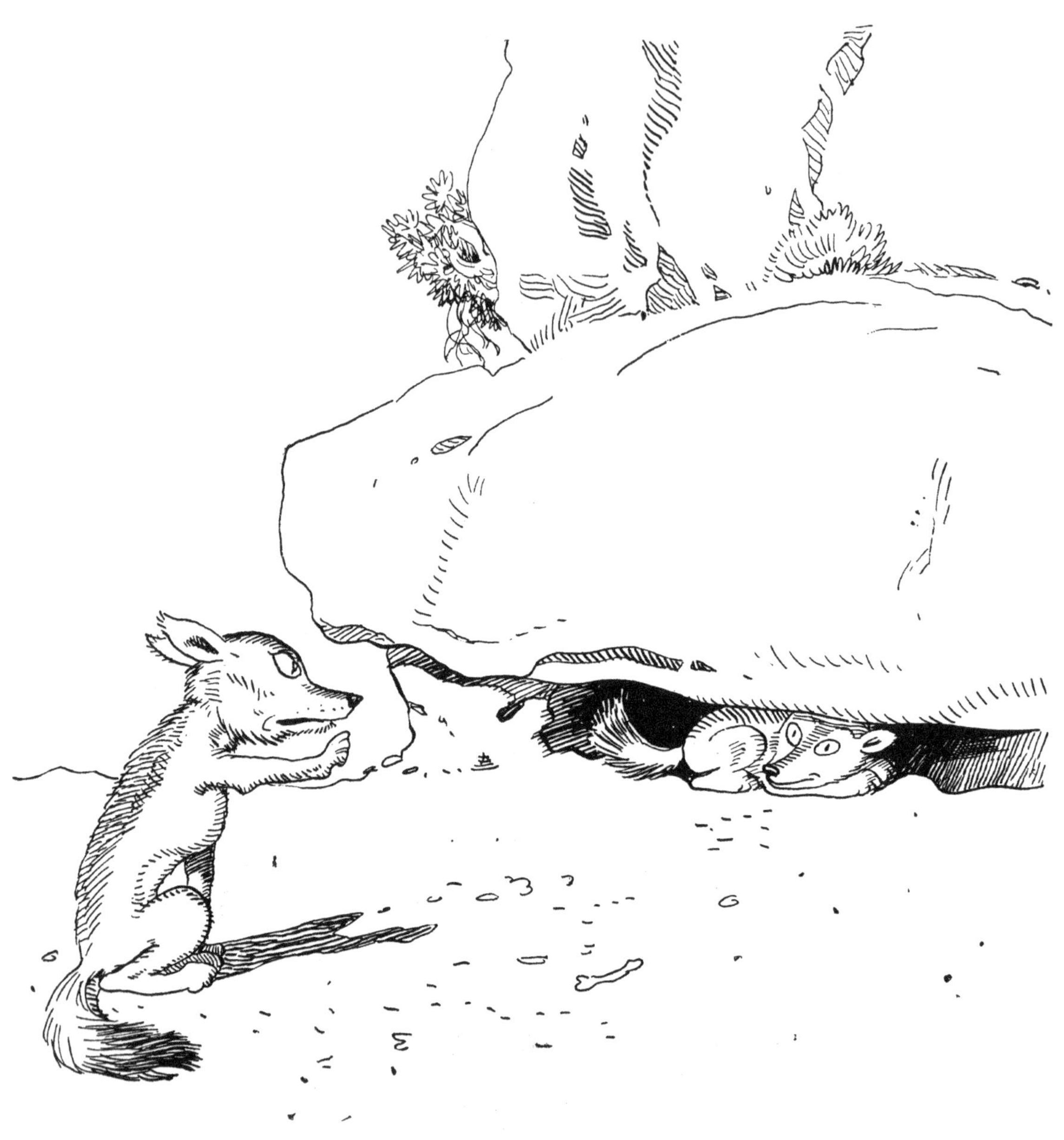

But when the little Coy-o-te is having the bestest play,
Mrs. Coy-o-te puts him to bed to sleep the whole long day.

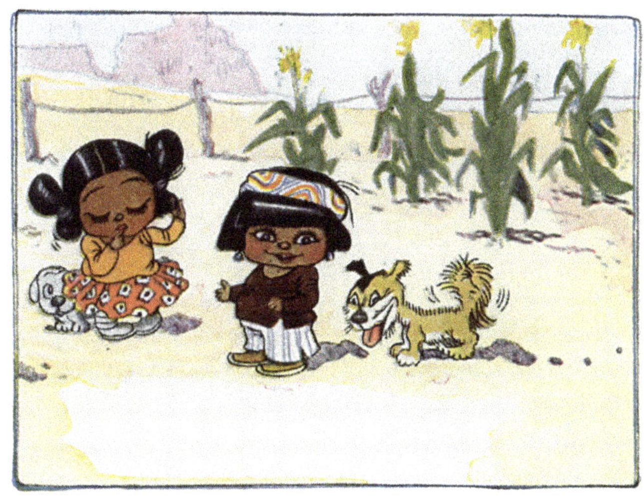

This kiddie's name is Ne-huck-oo.
He loves to mind his father.
He loves to mind his mother, too,
When it isn't any bother.

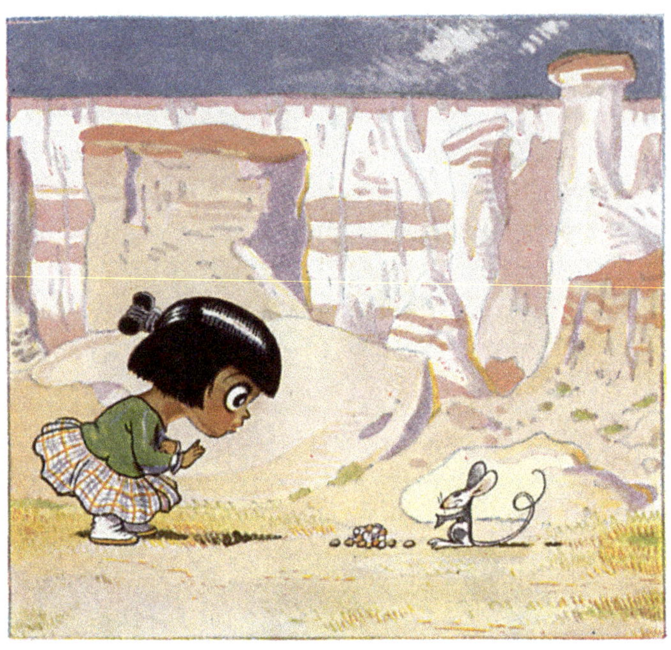

A Trade Rat had a habit of stealing things
away,
But always he replaced them with something else next day.
He took away some candy Ne-sa had hid-
den in a box,
But in the morning he brought back a
pile of little rocks.

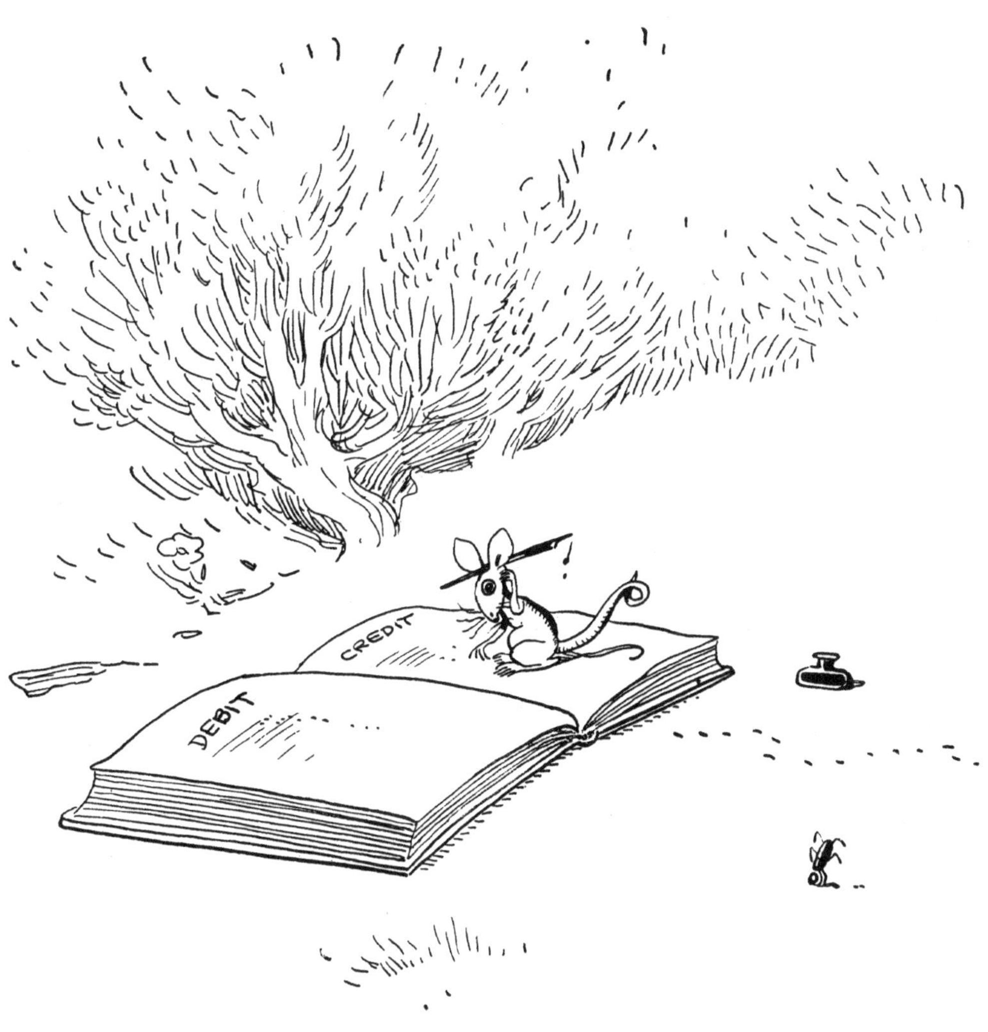

Before a little Trade Rat takes things of mine away,
I wish he'd tell me what he'll be bringing back for pay.

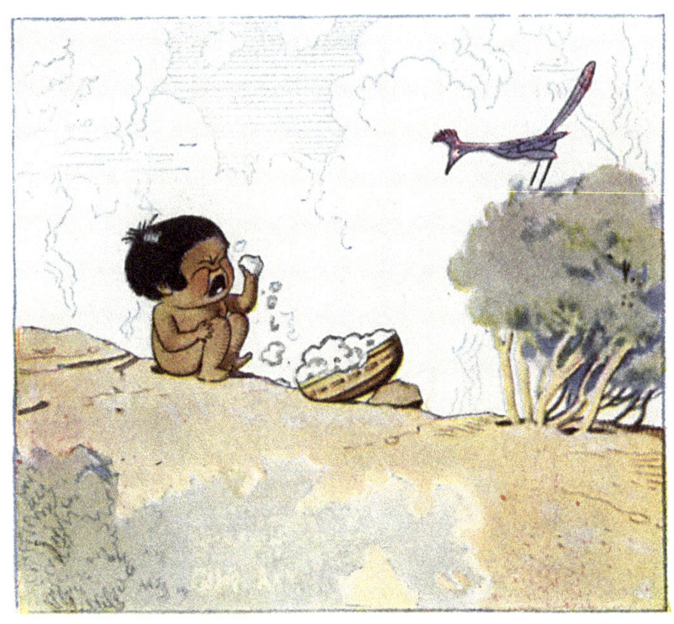

Little Hopi,
Hands soapy,
Finger, eye,
Oh, my!

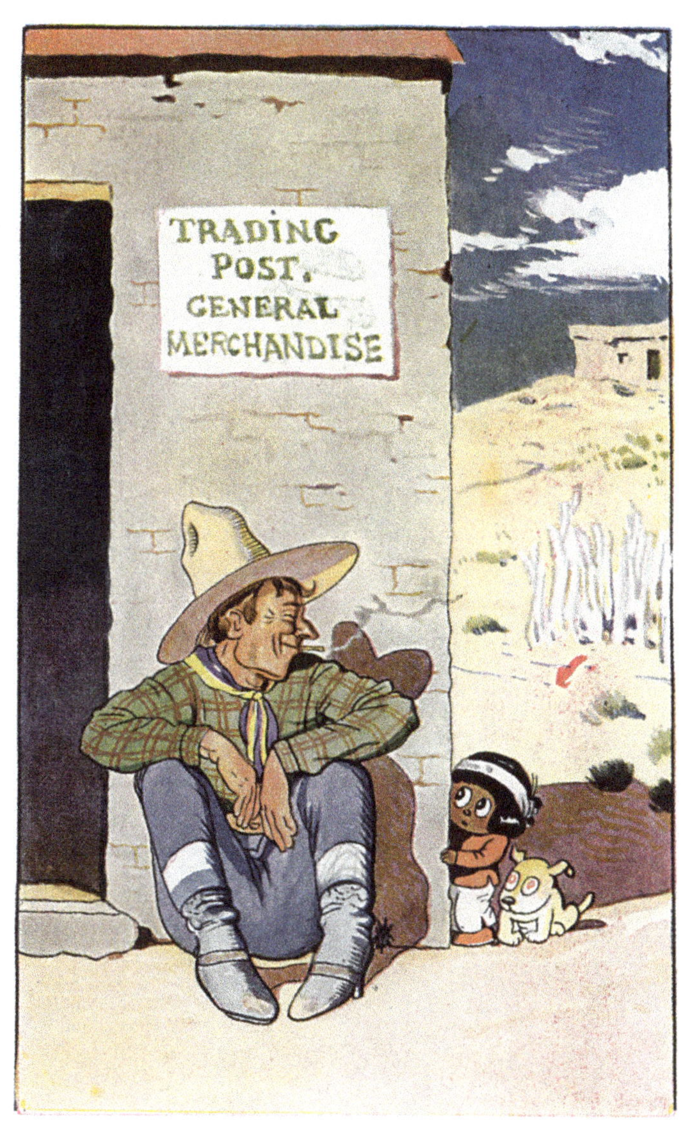

The cowboy at the trader's store
is big an' rough,
With word an' gun he's always
very handy.

But Ne-wa knows that if he
waits here long enough
He's sure to get a fine big piece
of candy.

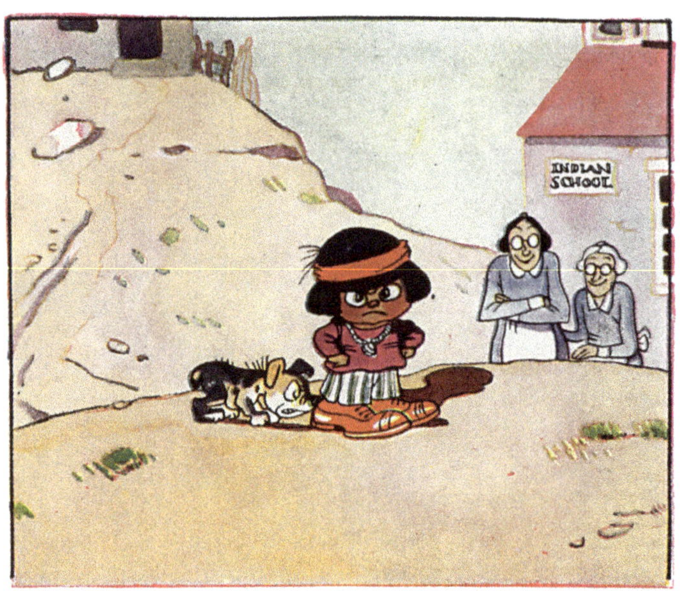

These pale-face shoes do not please Na-
ta-tim,
They're hot an' big an' very heavy, too.
He'll take 'em off when they quit watch-
in' him,
An' I don't blame him very much, do
you?

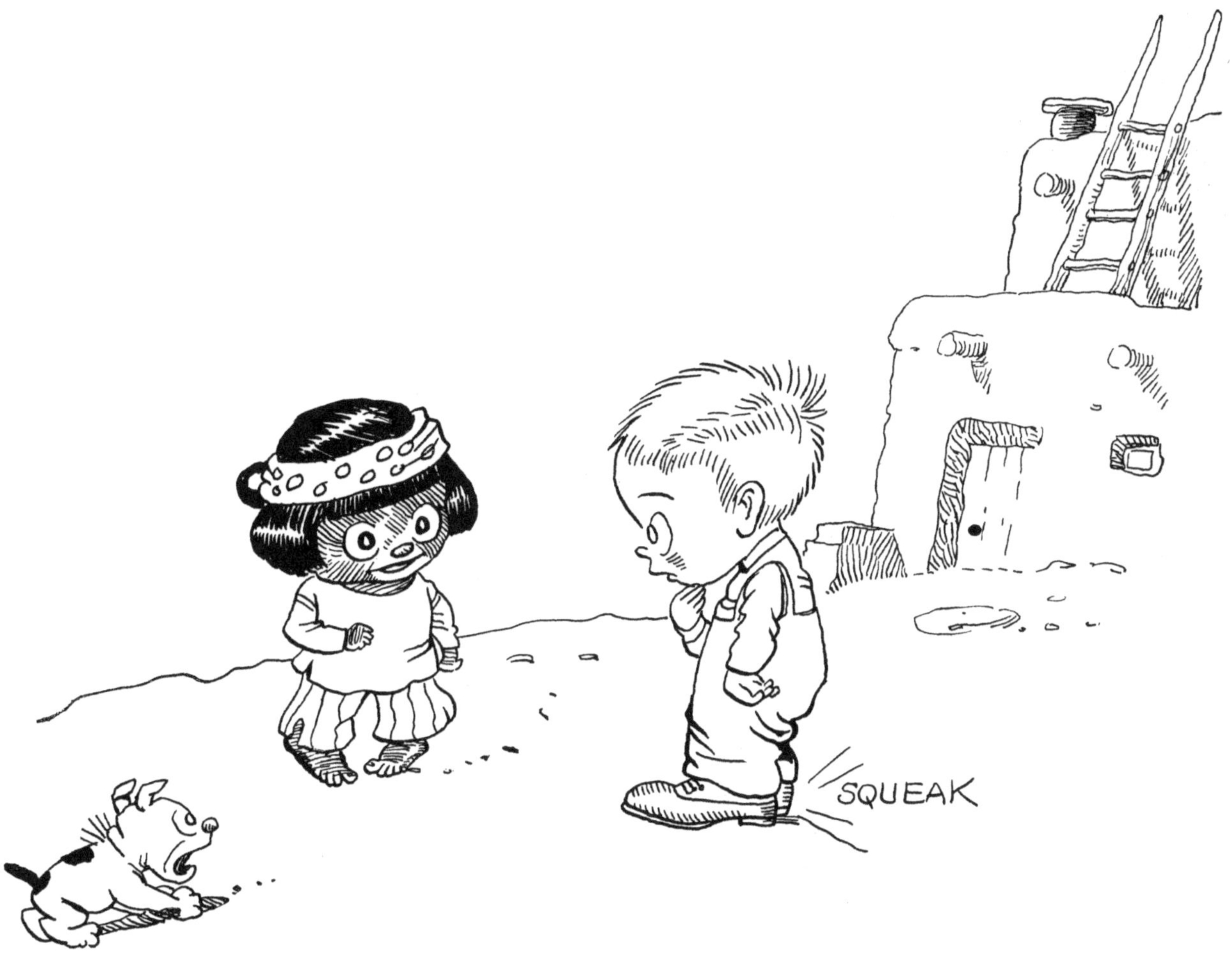

If I want to play and my shoes are very new,
I'd rather be barefooted—wouldn't you?

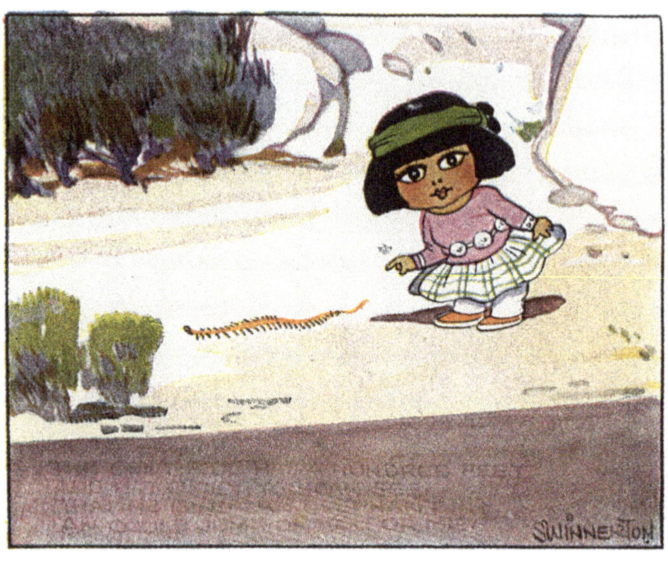

The Centipede has a hundred feet
And it's lucky, you can see,
That he is not an Elephant
An' could jump on you or me.

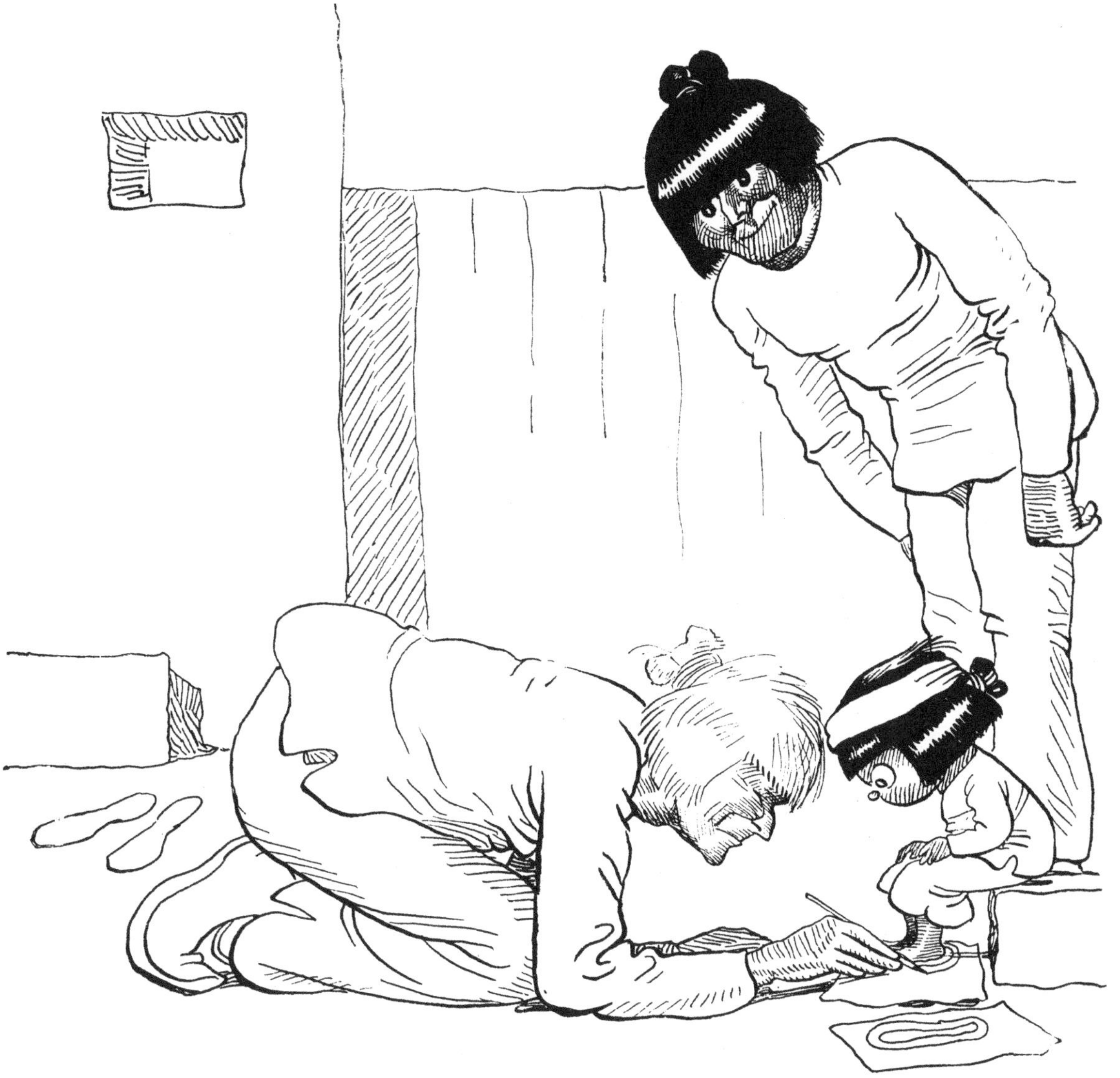

That we're not Centipedes should make our daddys glad,
And that our feet are counted just by twos.
It certainly would make them terrifically sad
If they had to buy us each a hundred shoes.

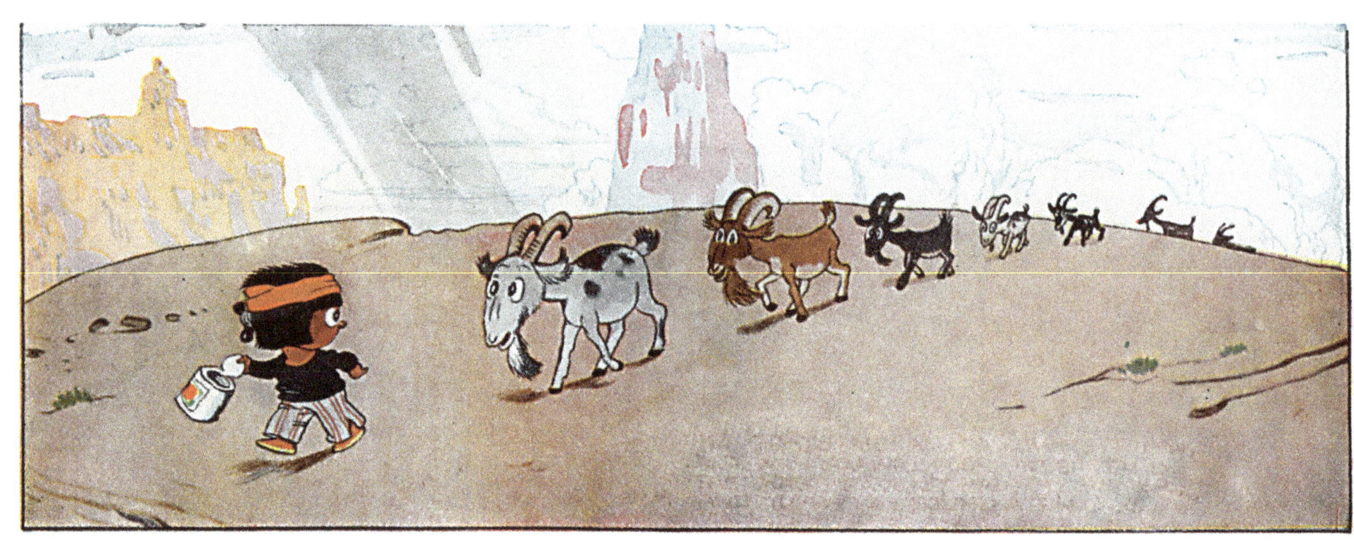

The Goats are all following Tuppa,
Just why you will soon understand:
The Goats haven't had any supper,
And Tuppa has found a tin can.

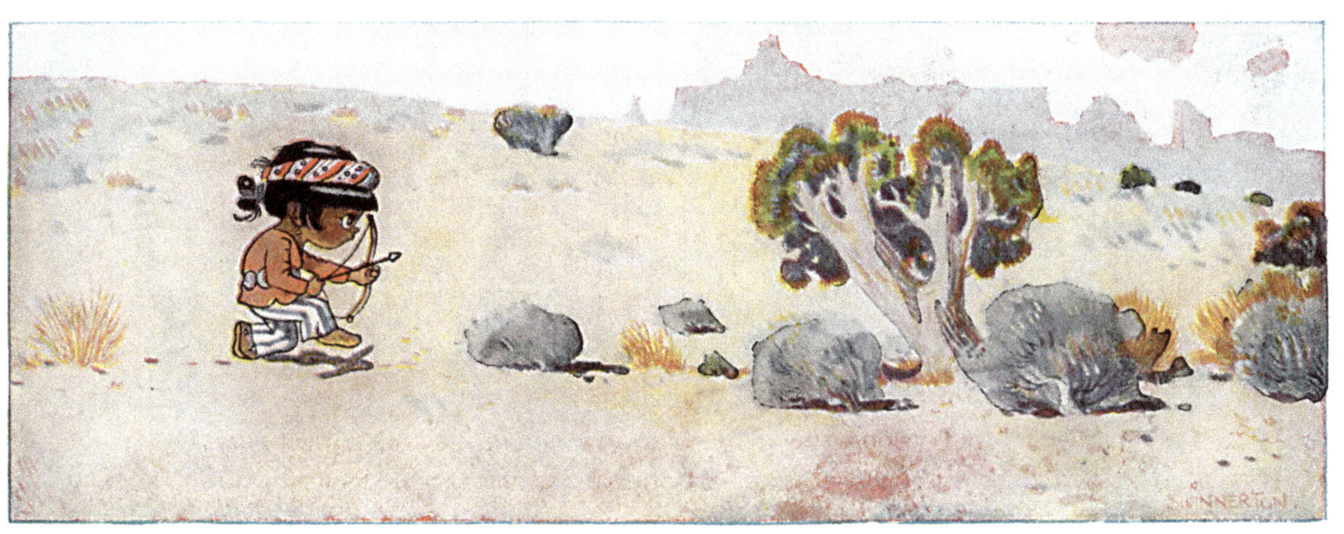

Where are the little birds and things we usually
see about?
There's not a squeak and not a cheep not even
from a sparrow.
They all know if they're careless and stick their
noses out
There'll be a lot of mischief done by Be-gay's
bow and arrow.

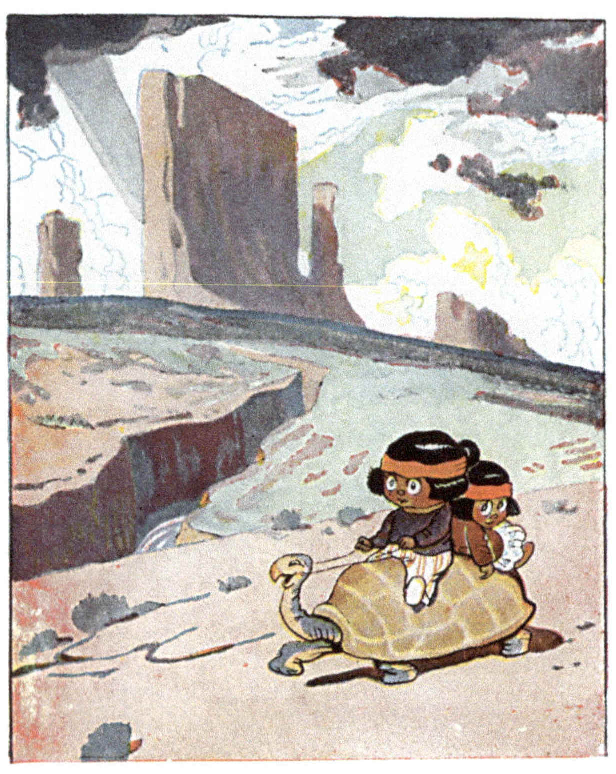

The Desert Terrapin loves to roam,
He travels the desert from rim to rim;
Yet never leaves his happy home,
Because it's fixed right tight to him.

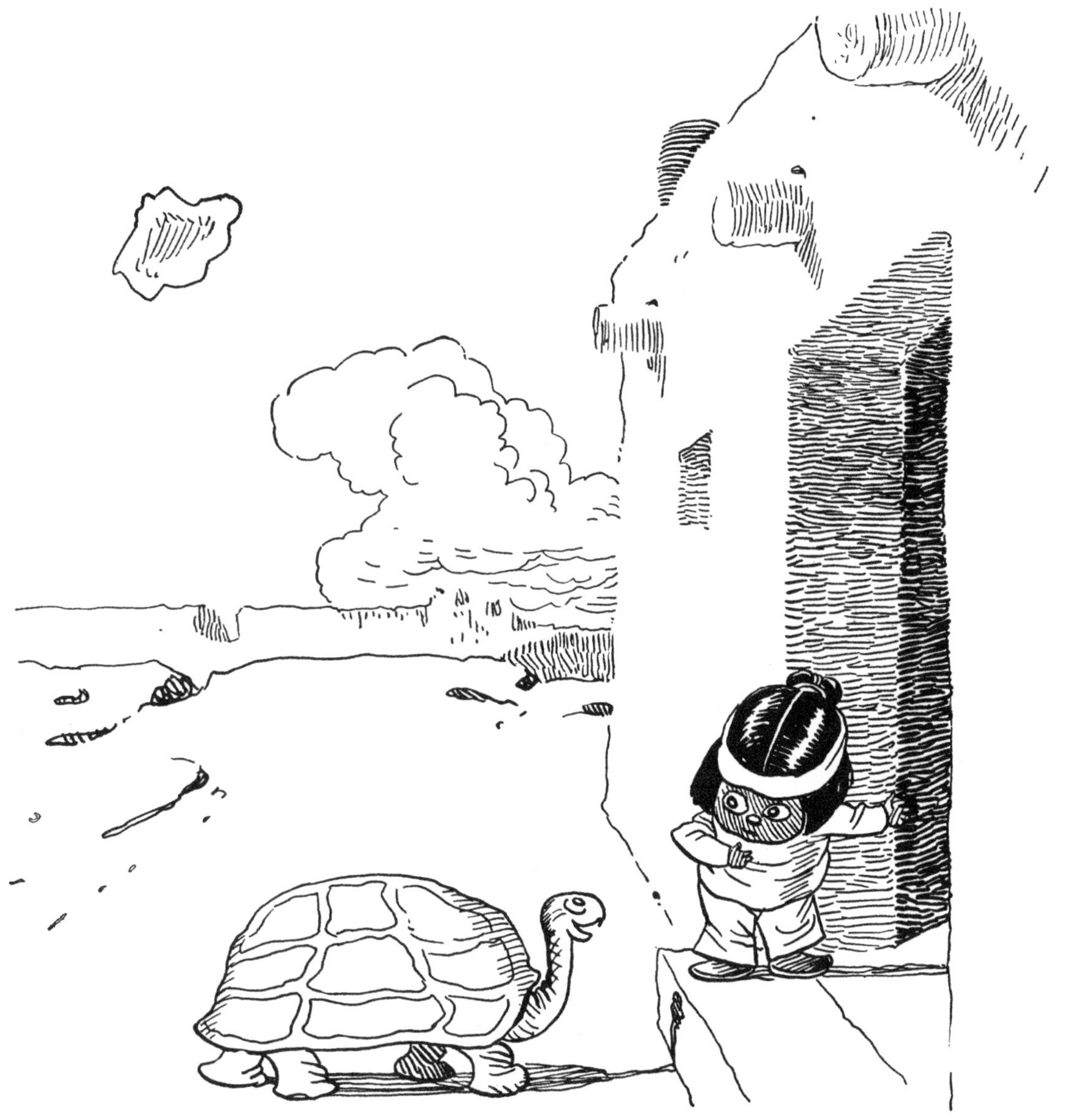

If this Terrapin were to call on you
The only thing that you could do
Would be to ask him in and say,
"Bring in your house and spend the day."

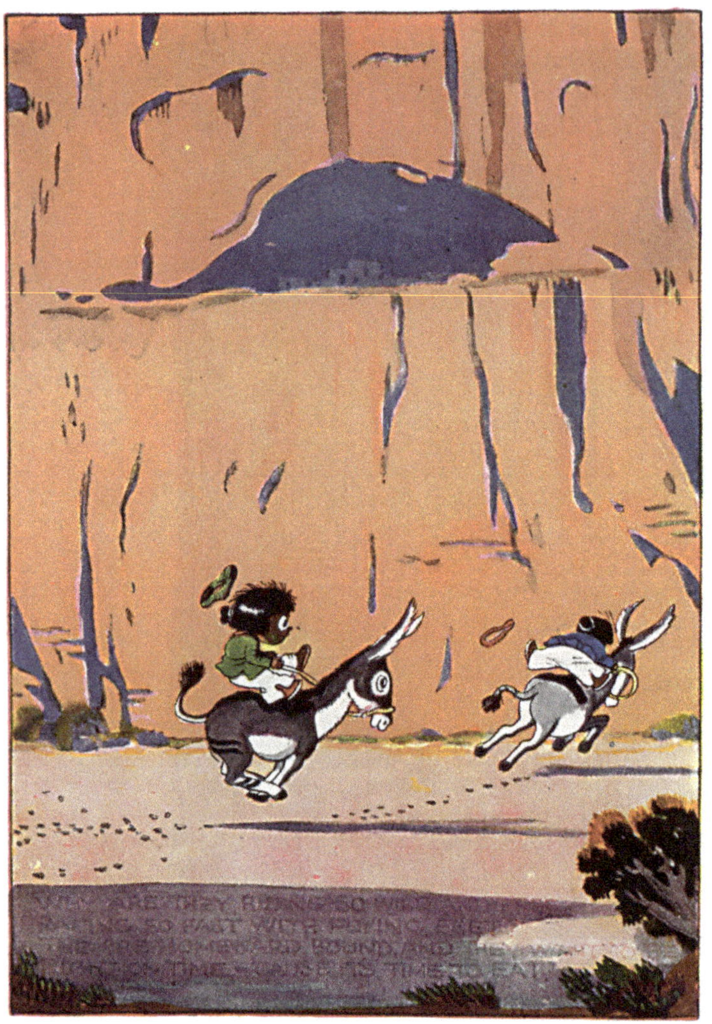

Why are they riding so wild and free,
Racing so fast with flying feet?
They're homeward bound, and they want
to be
Right on time 'cause it's time to eat.

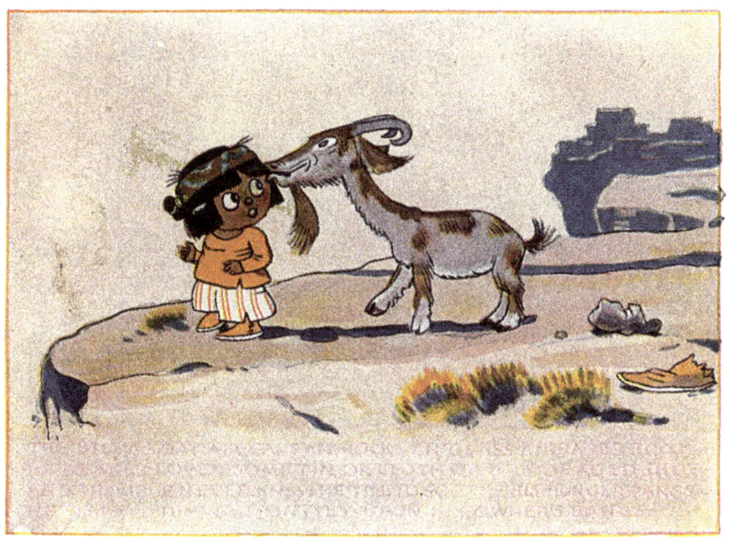

The Billy Goat ate cans an' rocks an' glass
an' paper too,
He dearly loved some tin or cloth or bits
of aged shoe,
And trouble never knew he till to soothe
his hunger pangs
He started dining daintily upon his own-
er's bangs.

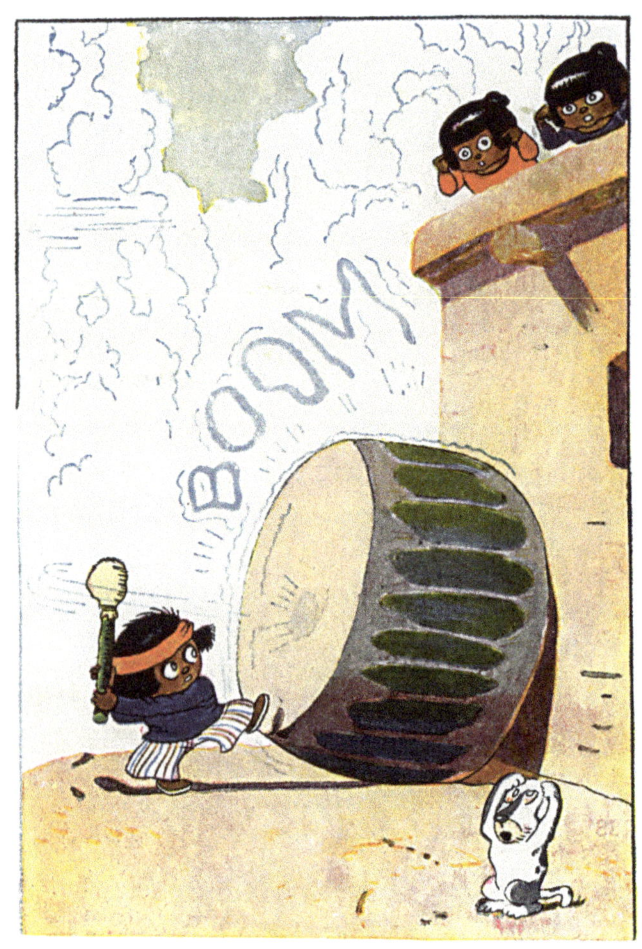

Cooking for girls and drumming for
boys.
(You'd think this drum would break)
My! Isn't this a great big noise
For one little boy to make?

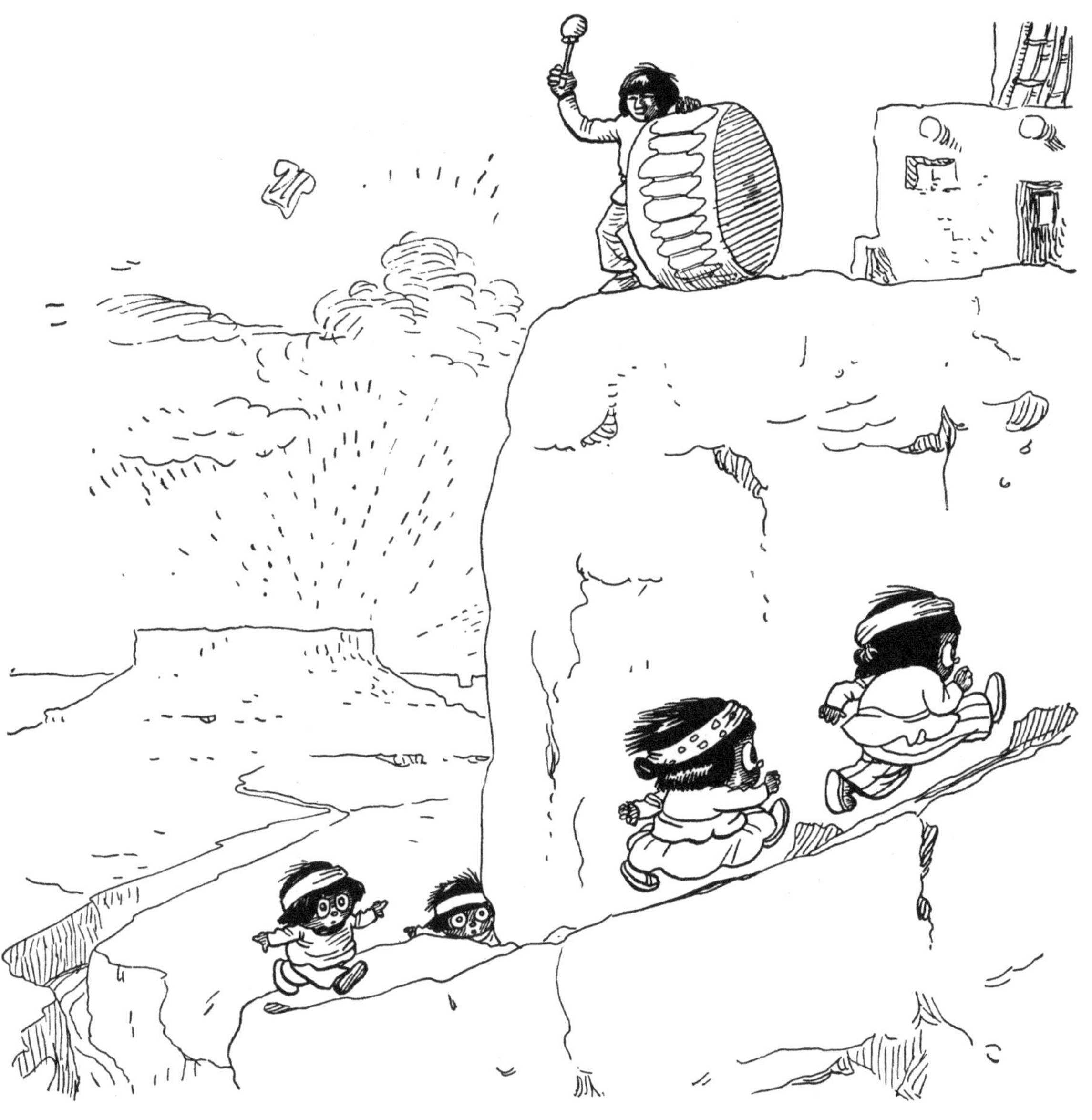

The Big Drum used to call for war,
And tribes have danced to its booming beat,
But its tones now carry loud and far,
Telling the little ones, "Time to eat!"

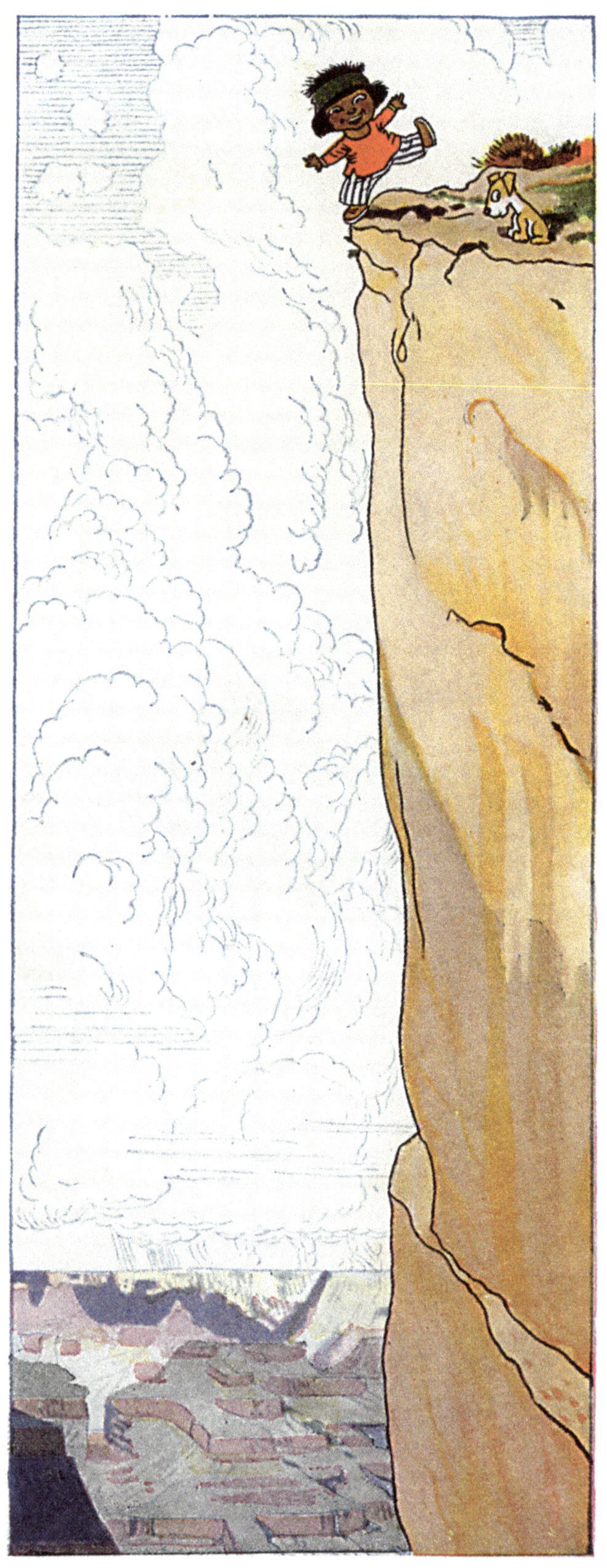

"It's a long way to Tipperary,"
As we recently heard it said,
But this wee Navajo
Would have farther to go,
He would think, if he lost his head.

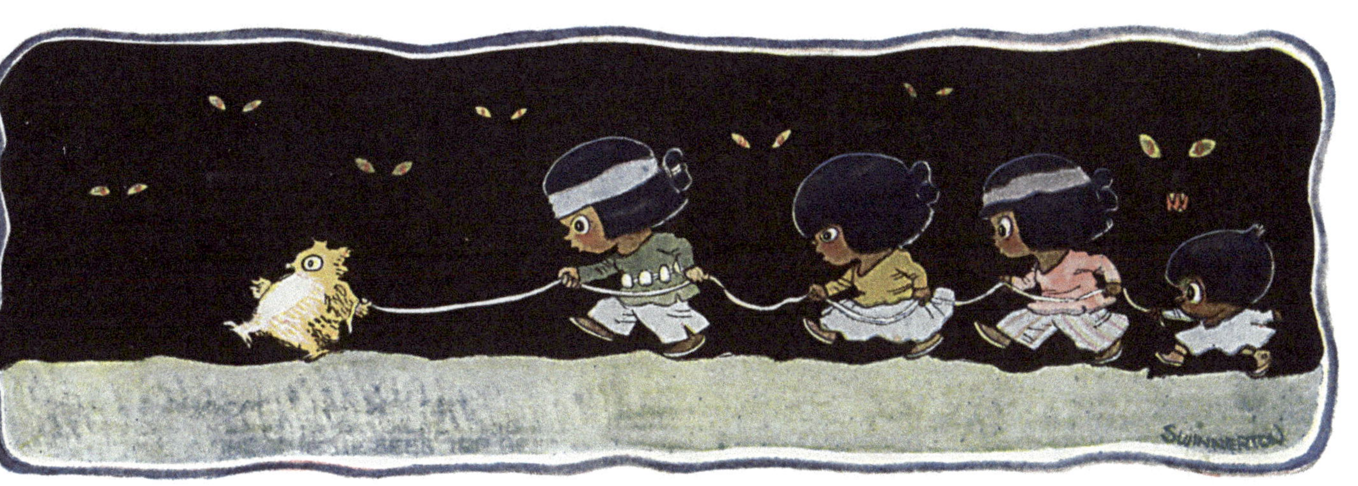

If you have to go some place at night,
And all is dark as a blackbird's vest,
Take an Owl along to guide you right,
'Cause that's the time he sees the best.

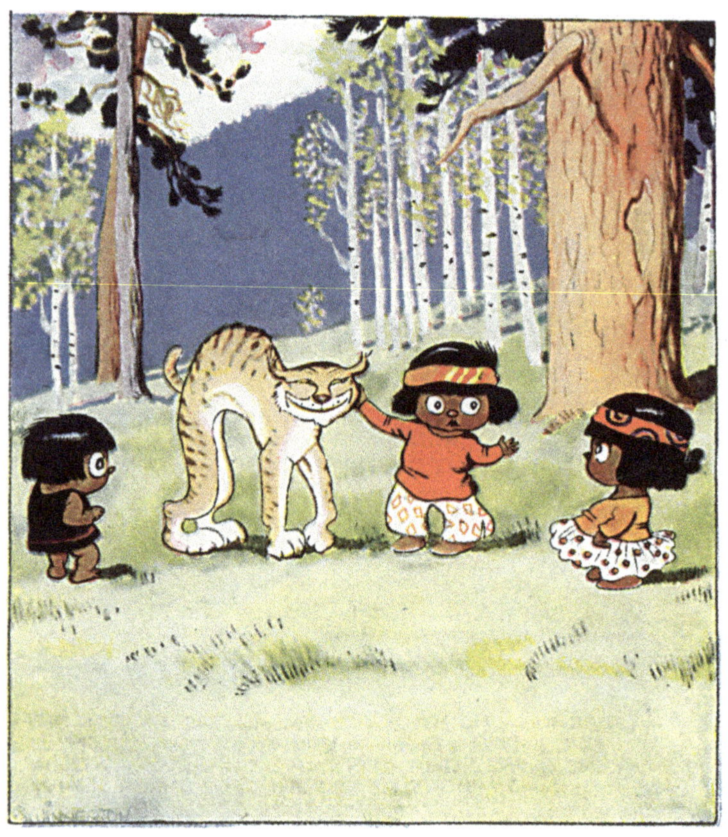

The Robert Cat, called wild (which is
unfair),
Is proud and kind and always on the job,
And only snarls and spits and claws the
air
When folks who hardly know him call
him Bob.

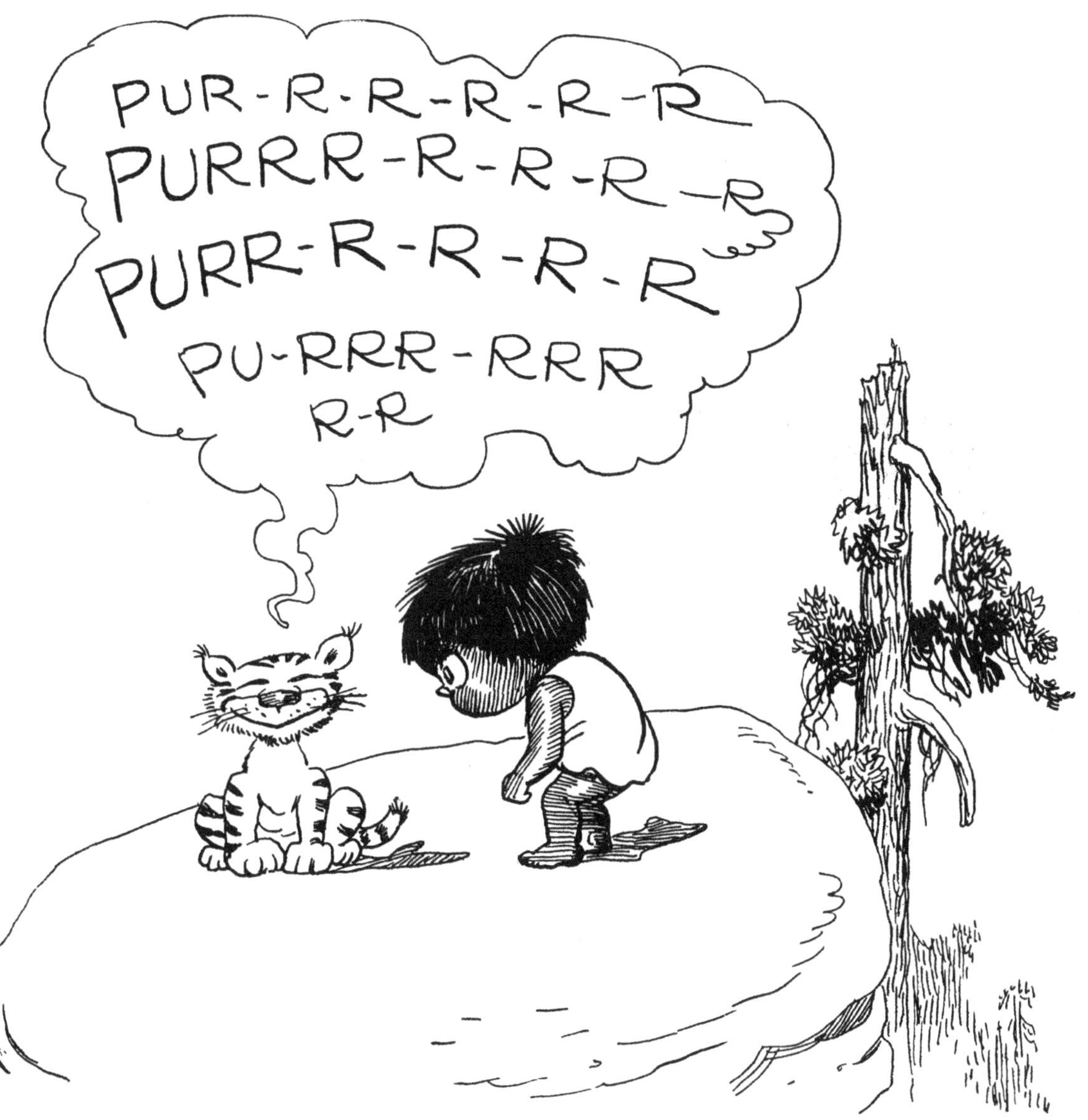

If you see a li'l' ole Bob-kitten
Go up and praise his fur,
Then go closer you won't be bitten,
He will only Purr an' Purr an' Purr.

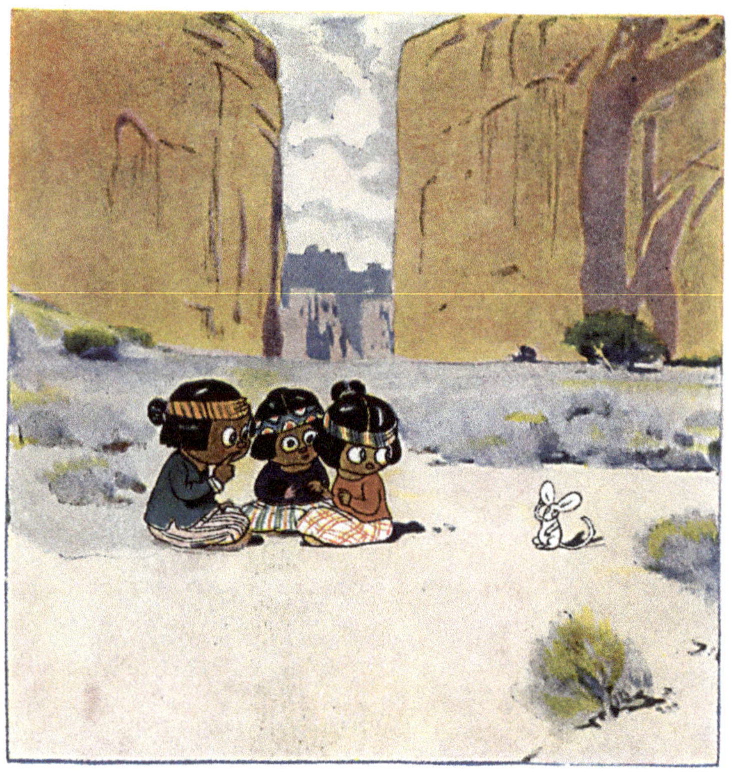

"A little Bird has told me,"
Is what folks often say,
When you ask them how
They found a secret out.
In Hopi-land news travels
In quite another way—
Can you guess who carries
Secrets round about?

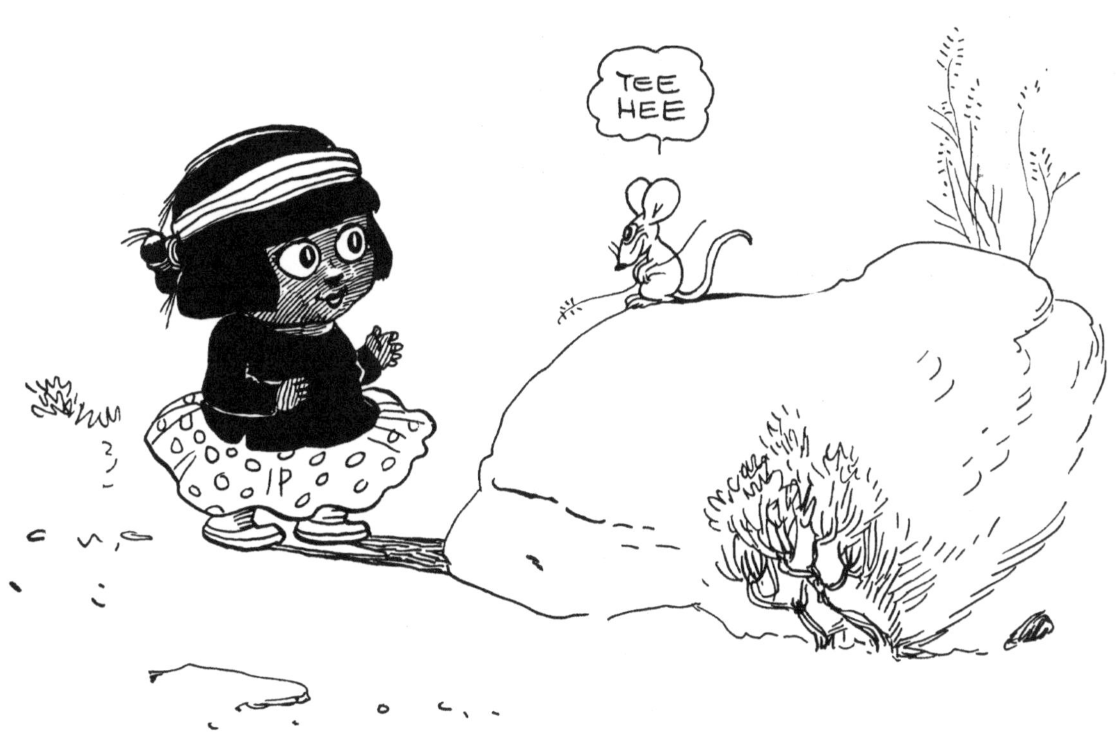

A Field Mouse must be always joyous
It appears,
We've never known one to annoy us
By his tears.

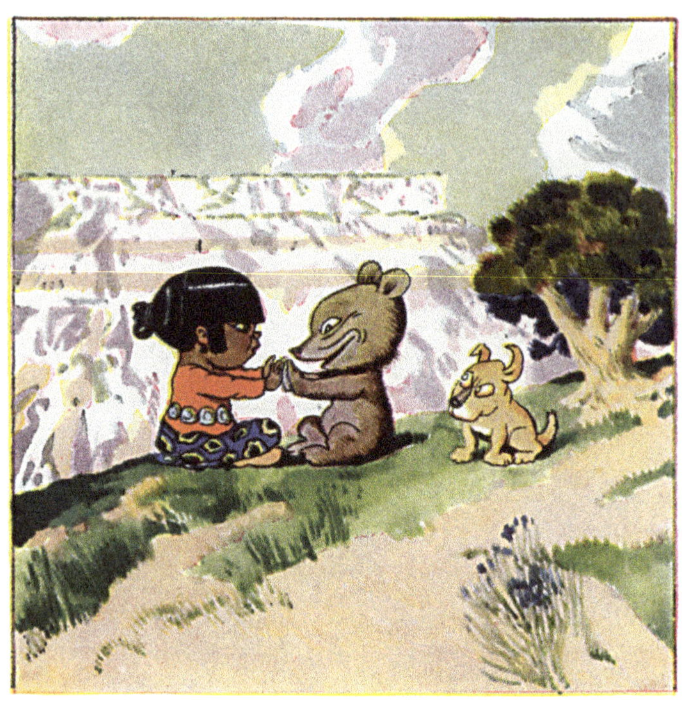

Bean porridge hot and bean porridge
 cold,
And bean porridge more than enough.
You've got to be careful in playing, I'm
 told,
With Bears, they're so awfully rough.

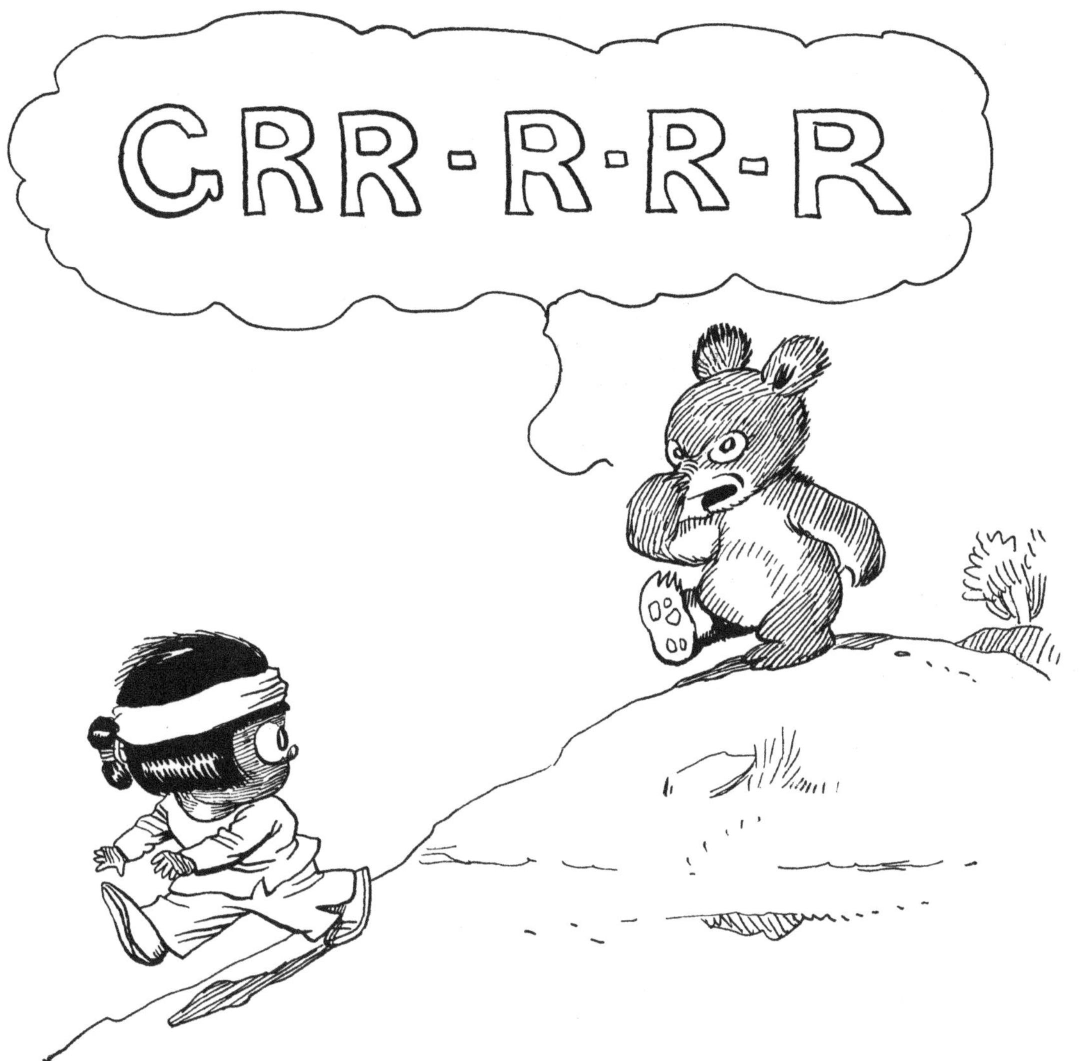

A little Bear will with you play,
And he will laugh at friendly blows,
But just the same don't get too gay
And hit him hard upon his nose.

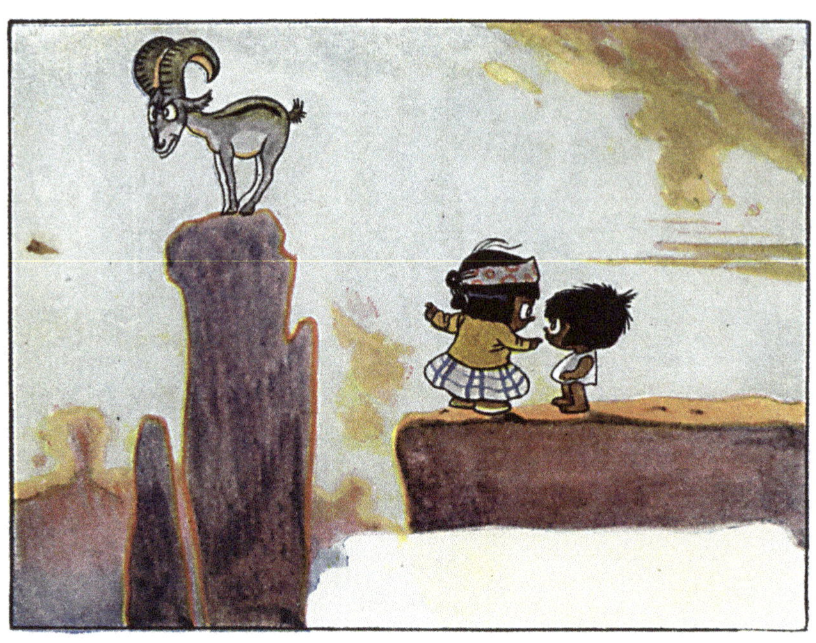

When night comes along, the big Mountain Sheep
Gets ugly and mean, so 'tis said.
An' I guess it is hard your temper to keep
If you have to take such horns to bed.

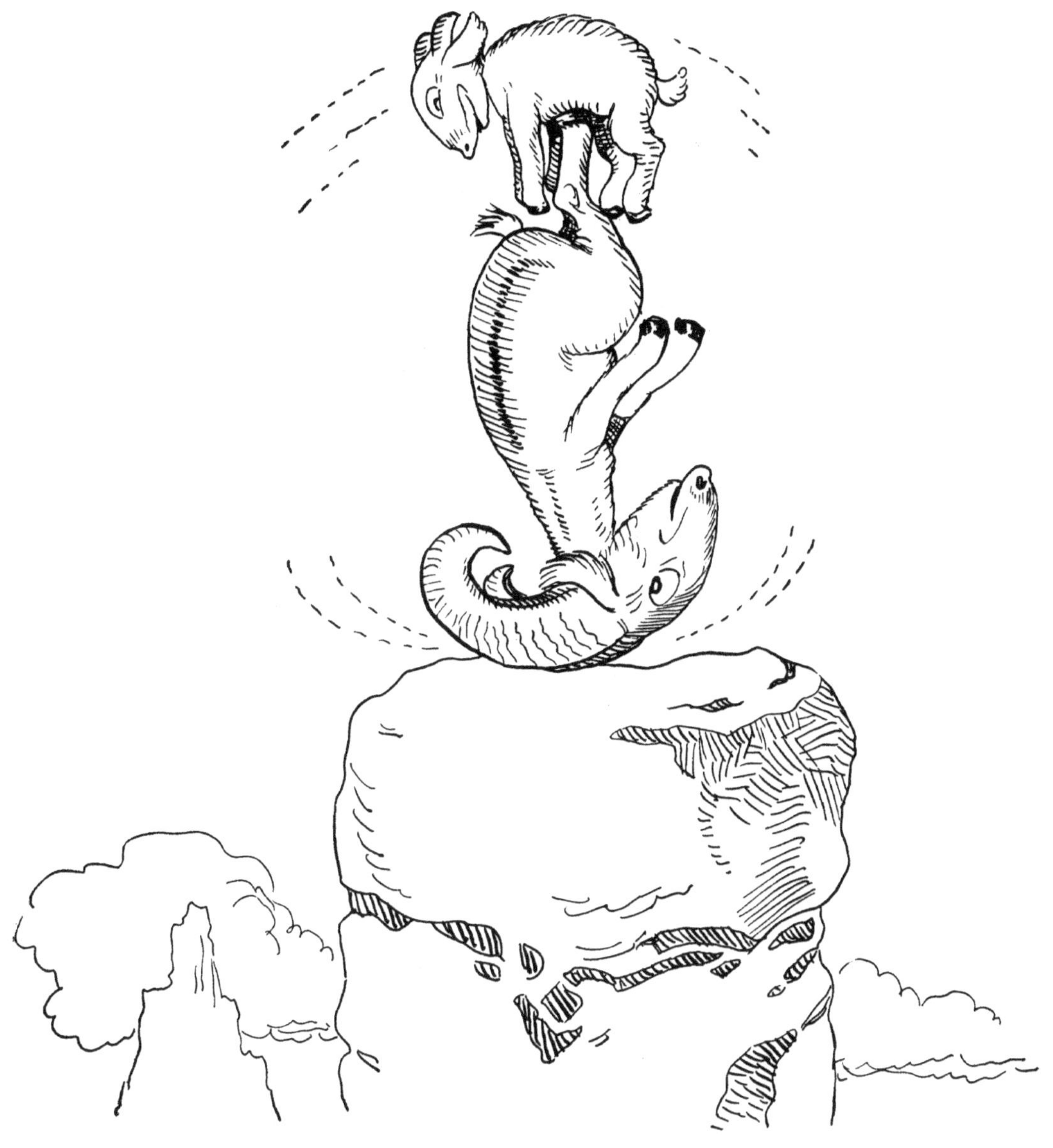

Rock-a-bye, Rock-a-bye,
Baby Mountain Sheep,
Up so high, up so high,
Safe on Mother's feet.

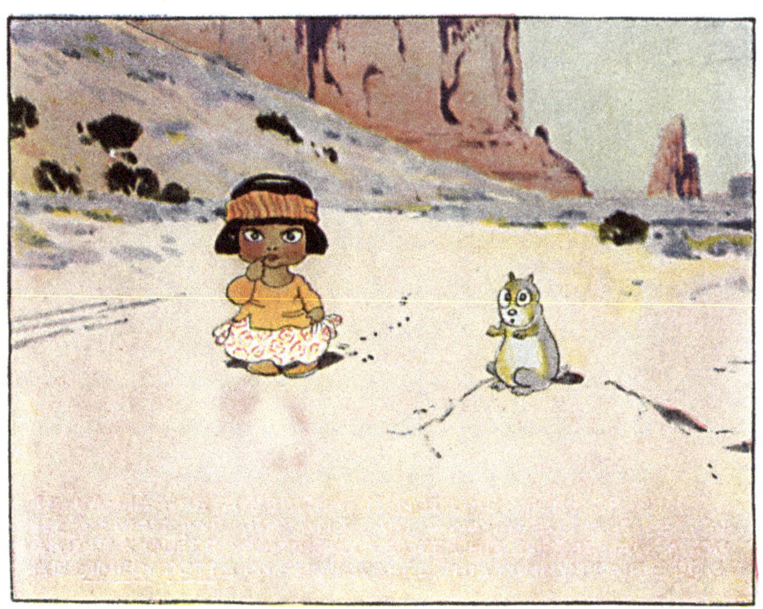

Te-ka-ma has a dog that is not like yours
or mine.
He's small and gray and darts away at
every little sign.
And if a queer, white face he sees, his eyes
are all agog.
He simply dotes on being scared, this
funny Prairie Dog.

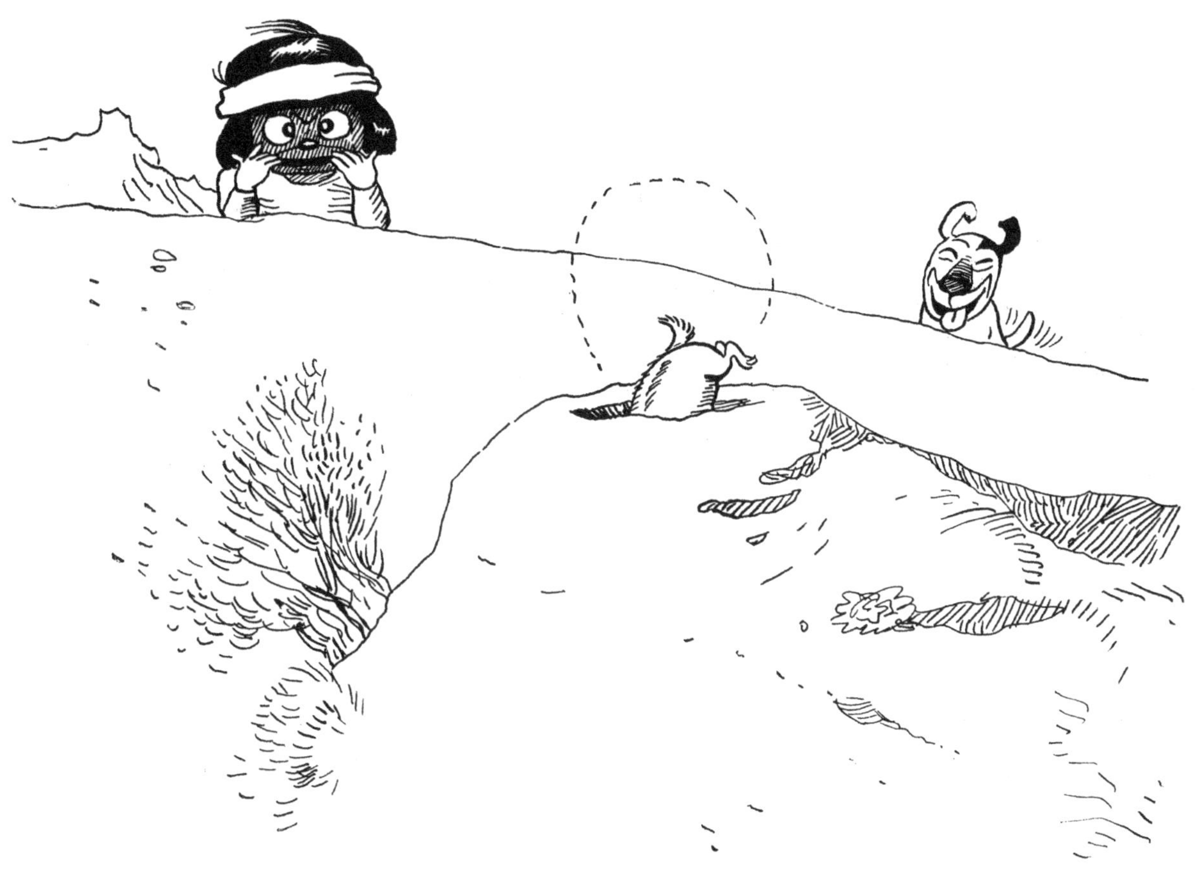

The Prairie Dog is scolding with a vim.
He sits up straight so very brave and bold,
But only make an ugly face at him,
And he will swiftly scamper down his hole.

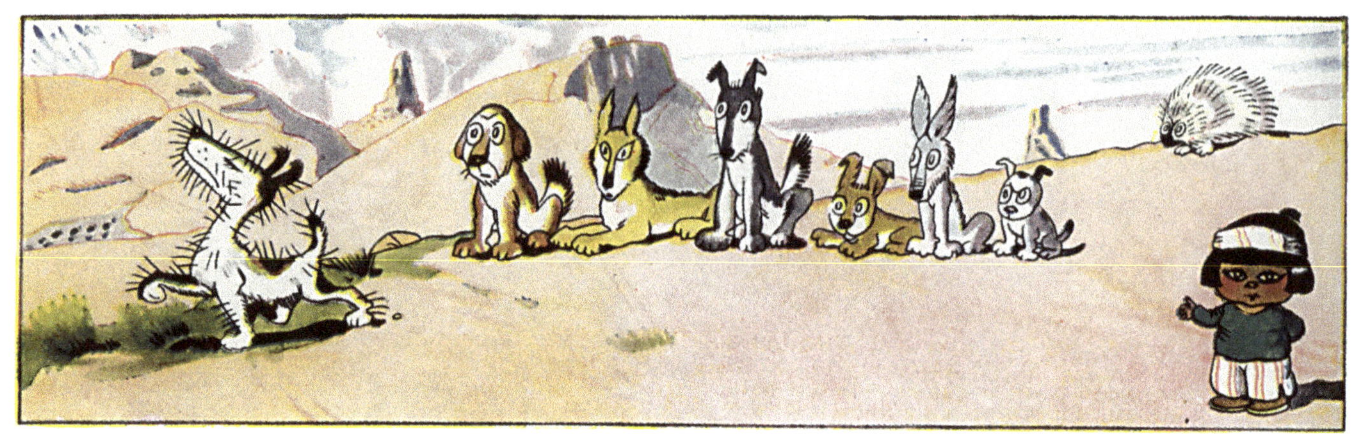

This haughty dog will not by look or sign
Even deign to notice any other pup,
He's just been playing with a Porcupine
And that's why he's so terribly stuck-up.

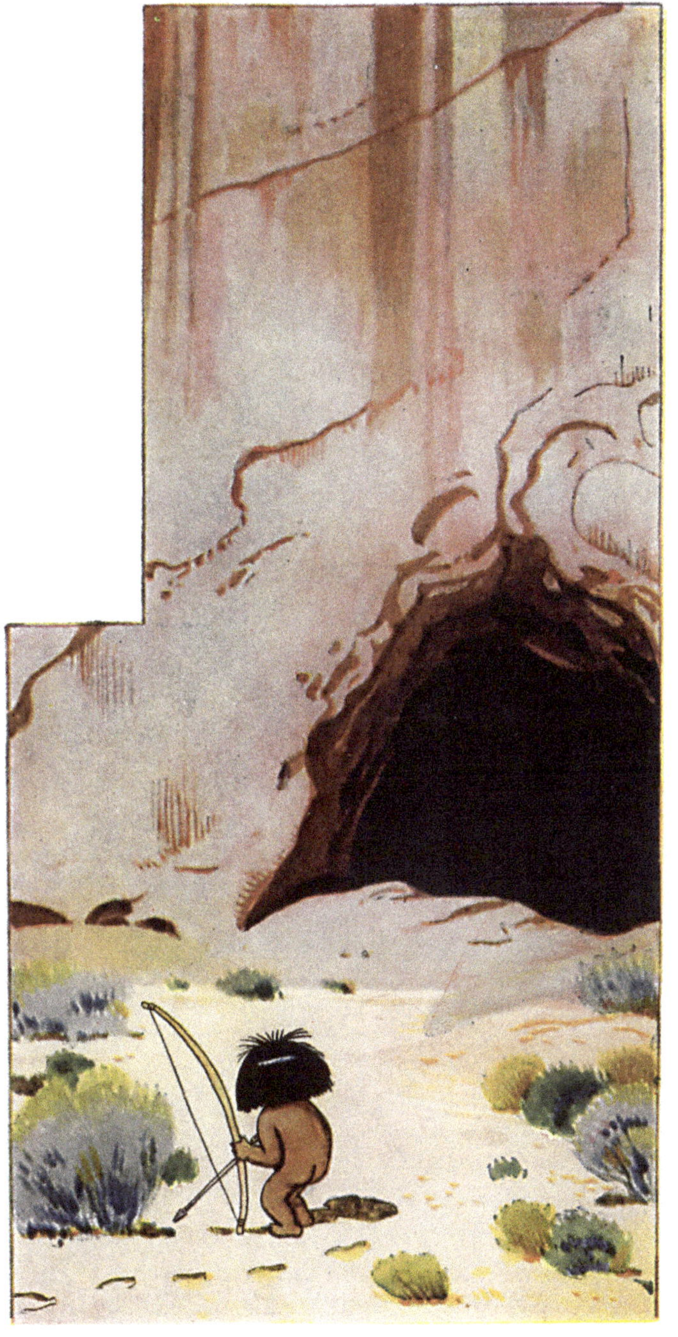

Things big an' awful an' growly
live in a cave like this,
So Hitt-a's come a-huntin' with
that cannot miss.
But the cave's so dark an' deep (it
go in a mile).
I think he'll turn an' go straight
back an' let 'em live a while.

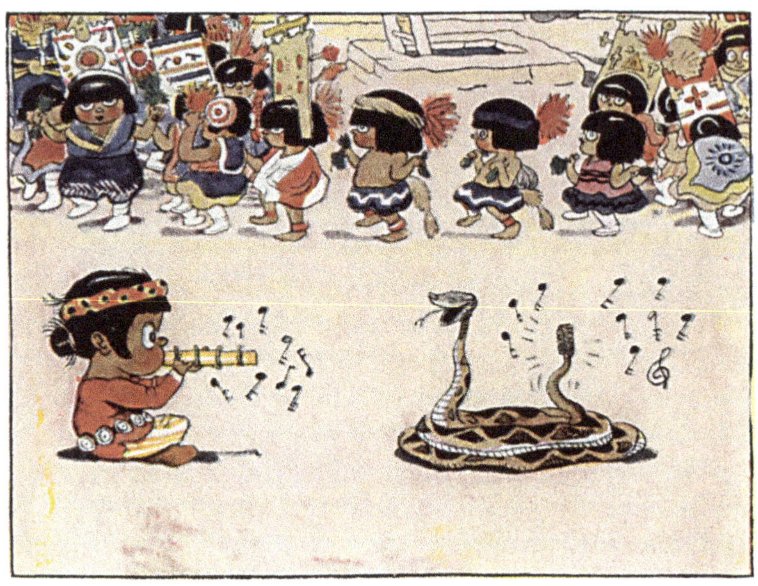

The Rattlesnake's rattle is supposed to
cause terror,
But don't form your opinion too soon.
This musical rattler would place you in
error
Because when he rattles he rattles a tune.

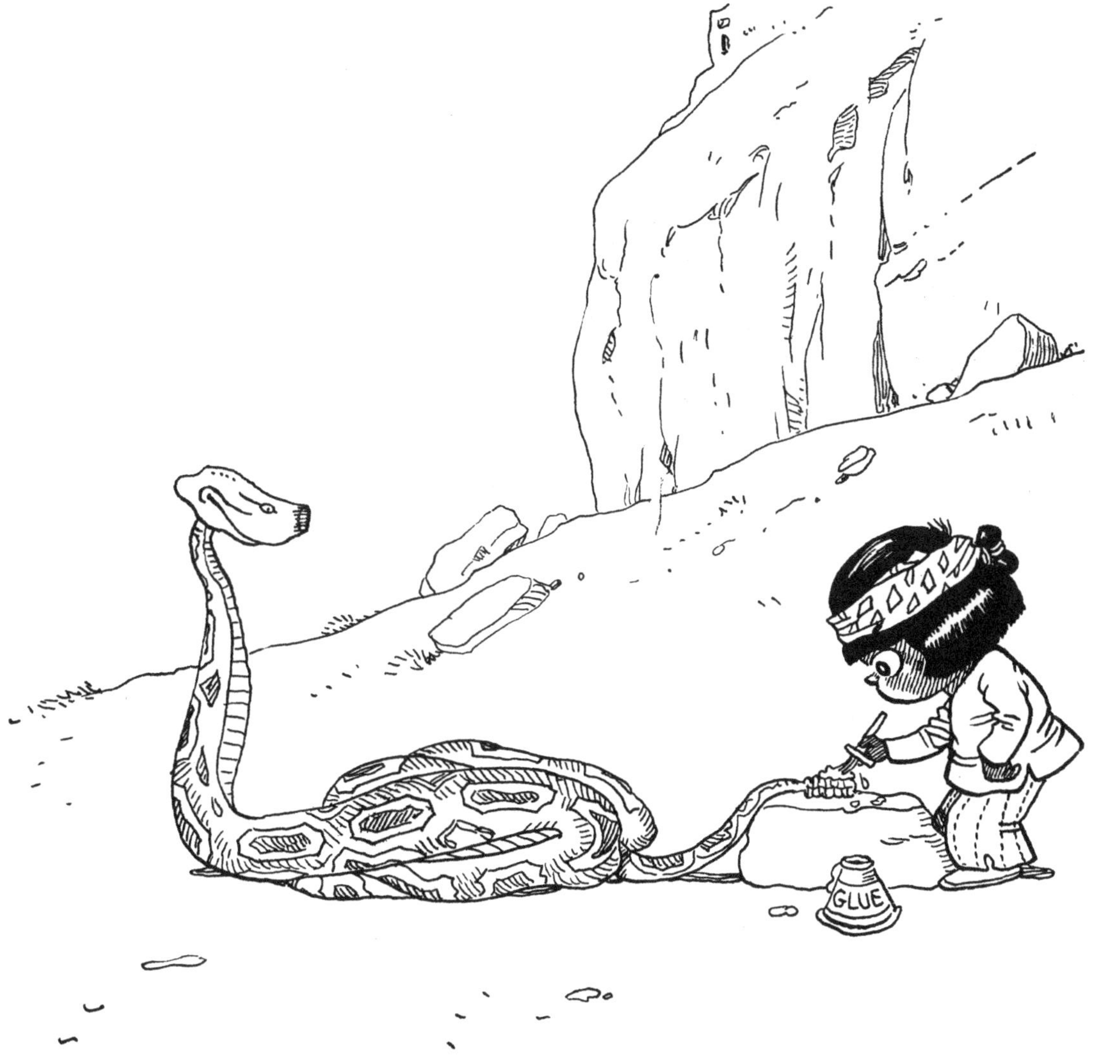

Some of this old Rattler's rattles are gone,
That's why he's having some false ones glued on.

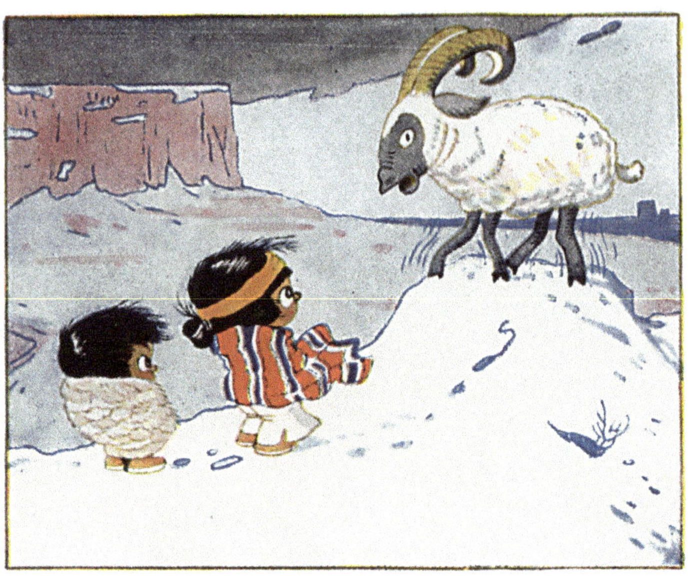

"I've a fine overcoat," said the Sheep,
"And the top of me warm it will keep.
But good gracious my ankles and knees!
Do get me some socks for them, please."

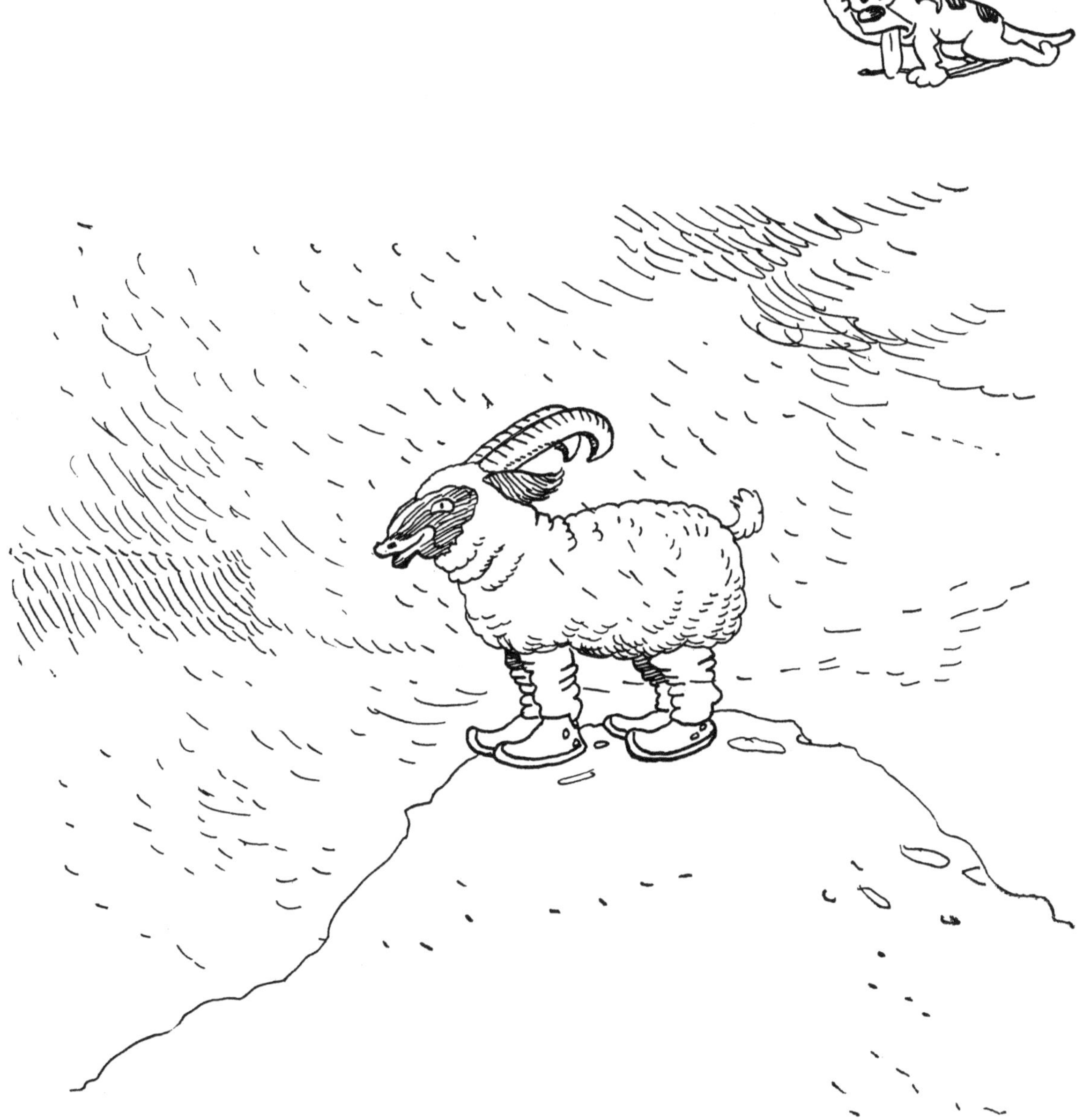

And now, you see,
Although the cold's intense,
He is comfy as can be
An' defies the ele-ments.

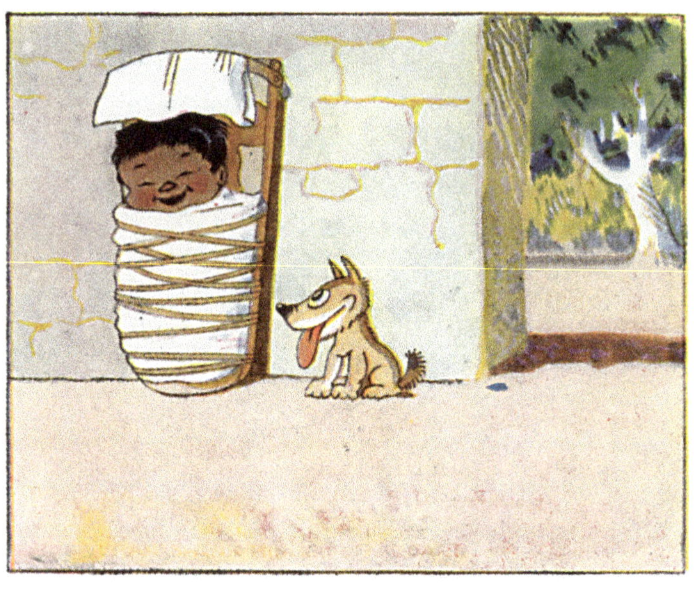

The pudgy Papoose laughs with glee,
He can act naughty as can be,
Because his mamma can't afford
To try an' spank him through a board.

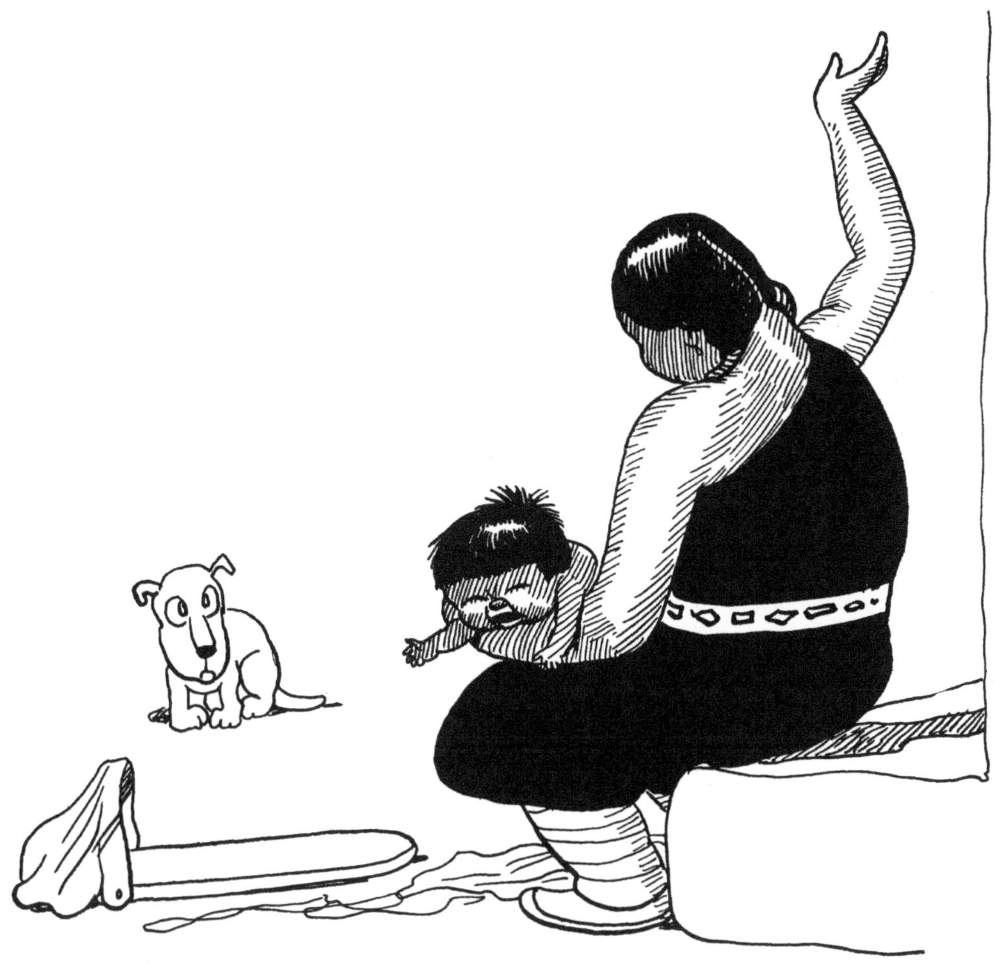

But he'd best be good and have a care.
Mother can quickly take him out of there.

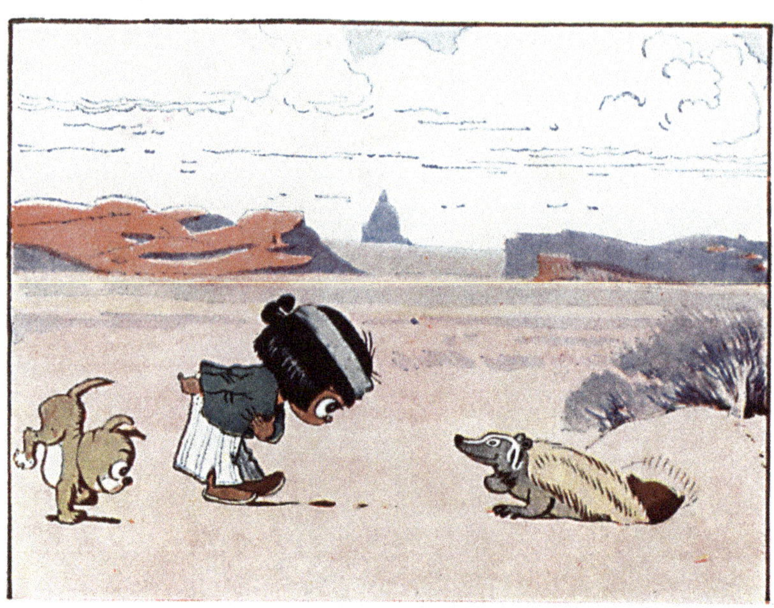

The Badger is always strong on class
Impoliteness is to him a sin,
So if in his door he has to pass
He gracefully faces you and backs in.

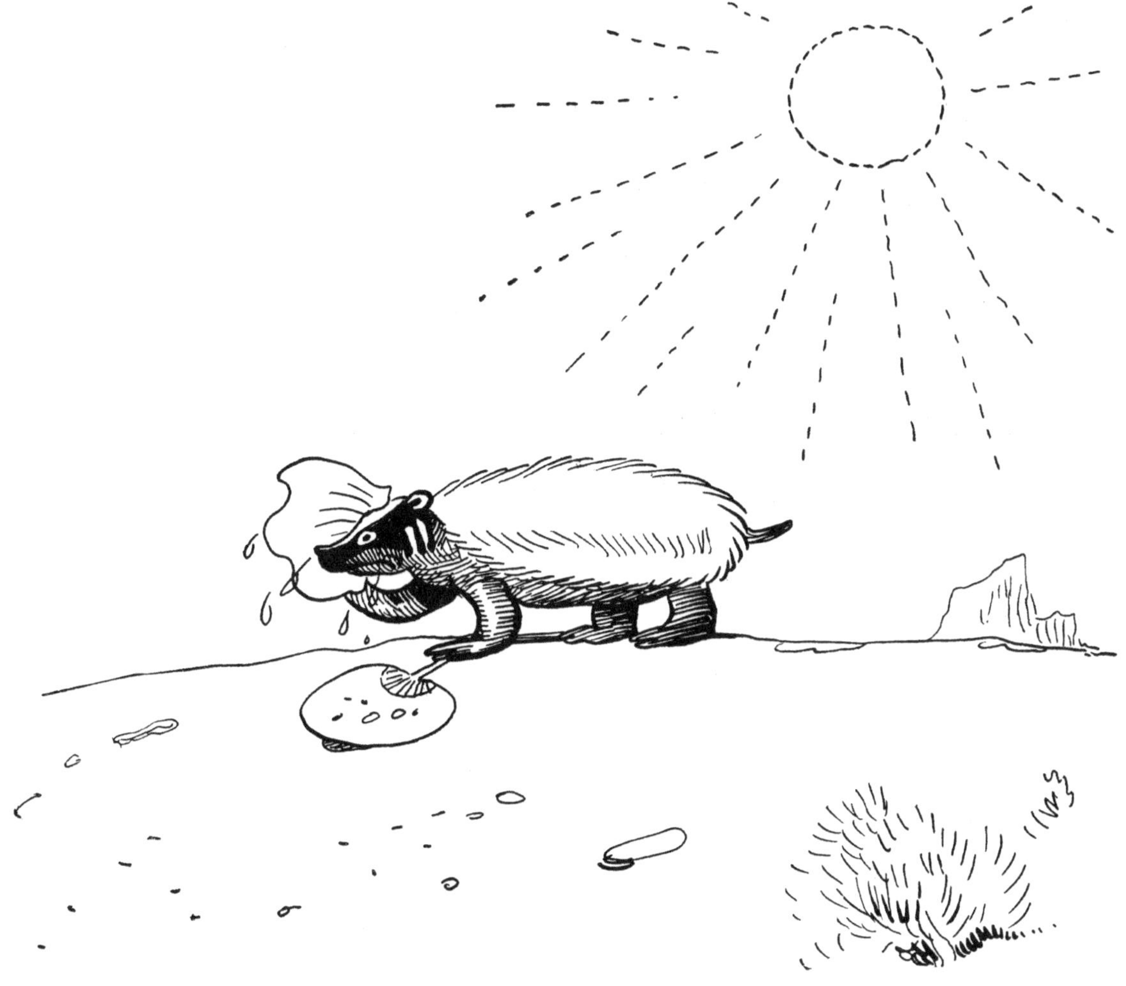

See the Badger's overcoat,
It's fastened to his back;
In summertime you'll note
It's uncomfortable to pack.

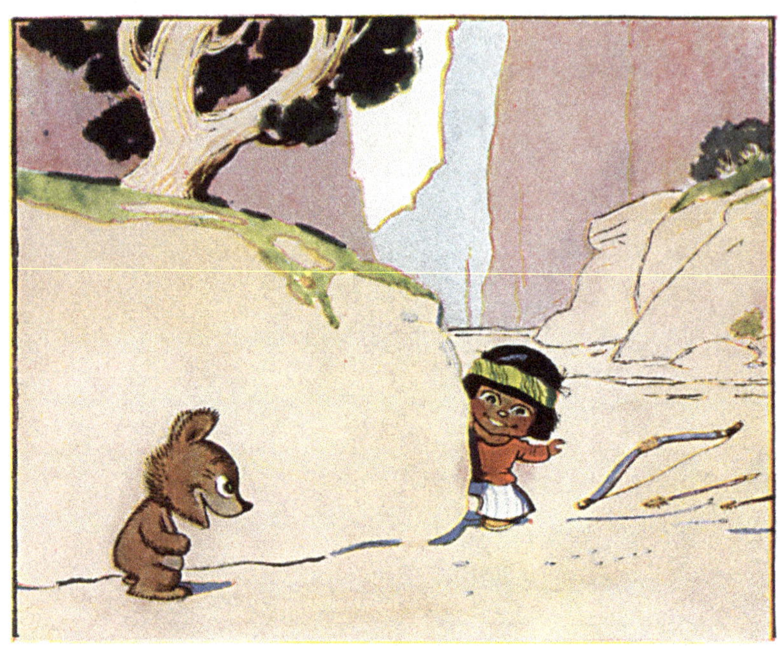

'Twas Hupa's hunting day; he'd tracked
something to its lair.
His intention was to kill it good an' dead.
But as soon as he discovered it was just a
Little Bear
He decided he would play with it instead.

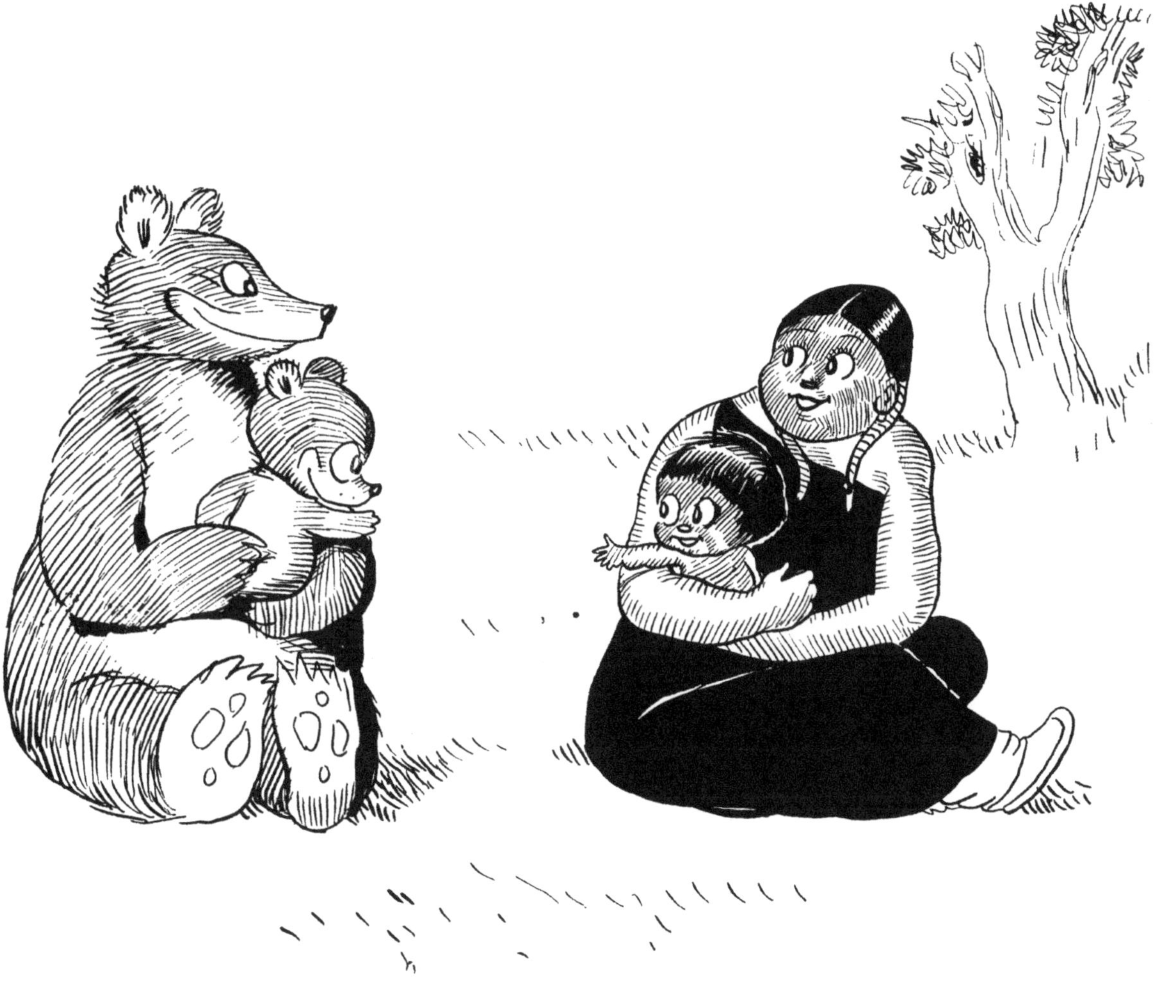

Little Bears and little Boys
Both of them are their parents' joys.

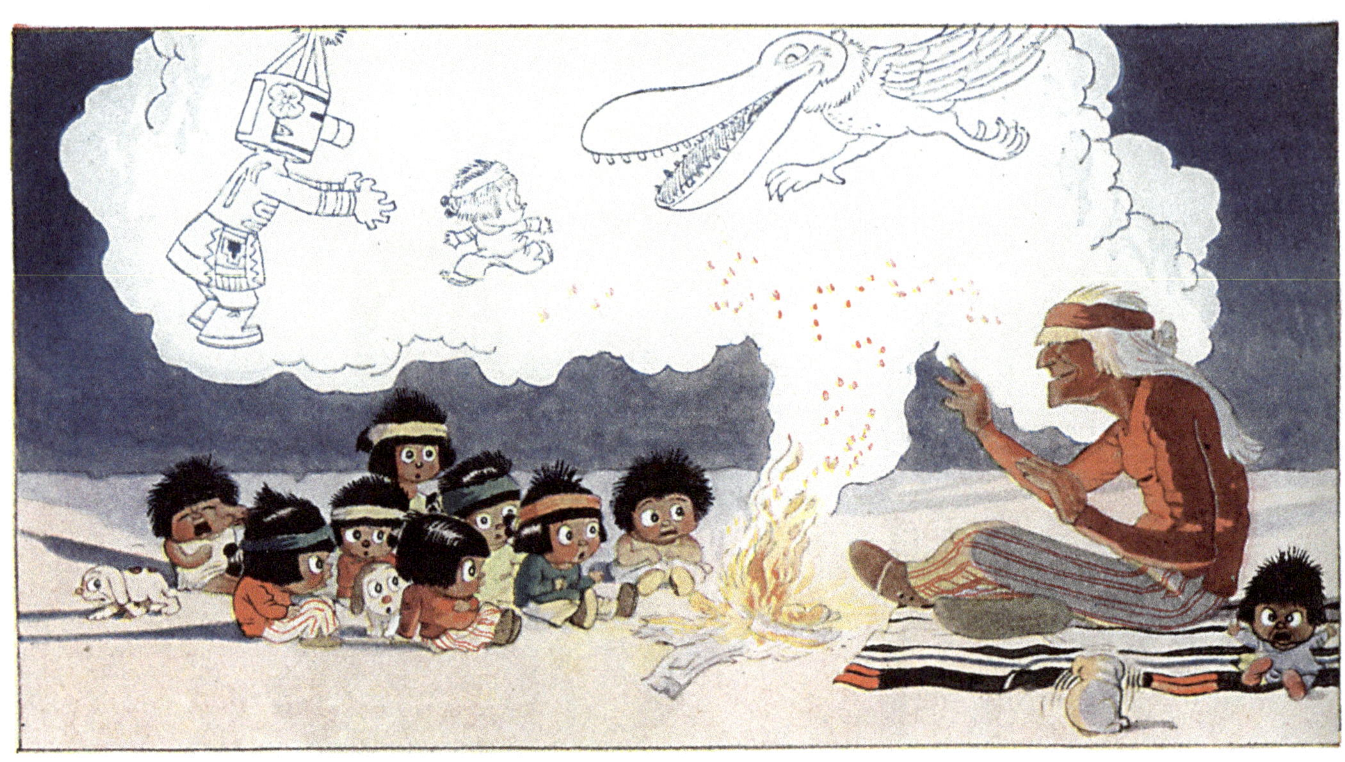

Shaddy's Gran'daddy is awfully old,
His hair is white as the river sand.
But OH! when stories are being told
He tells 'em simply GRA-A-AND!

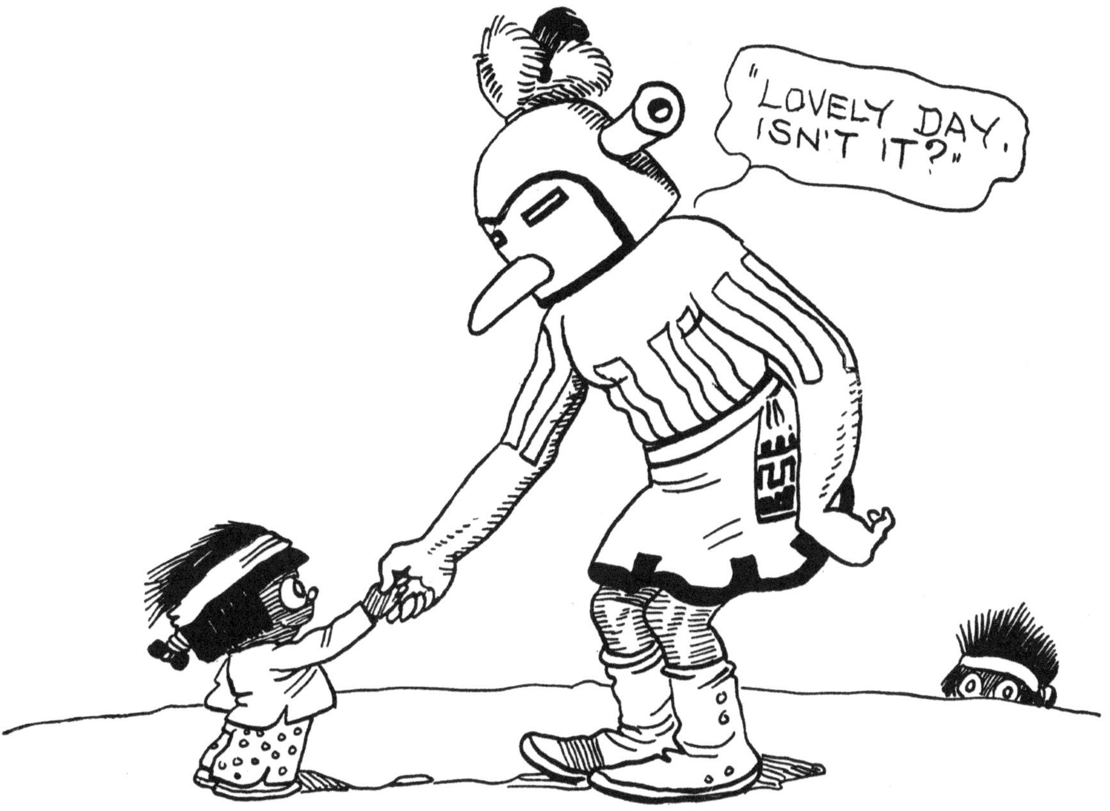

This is a friendly Bogie-man,
He'll even shake you by the hand.

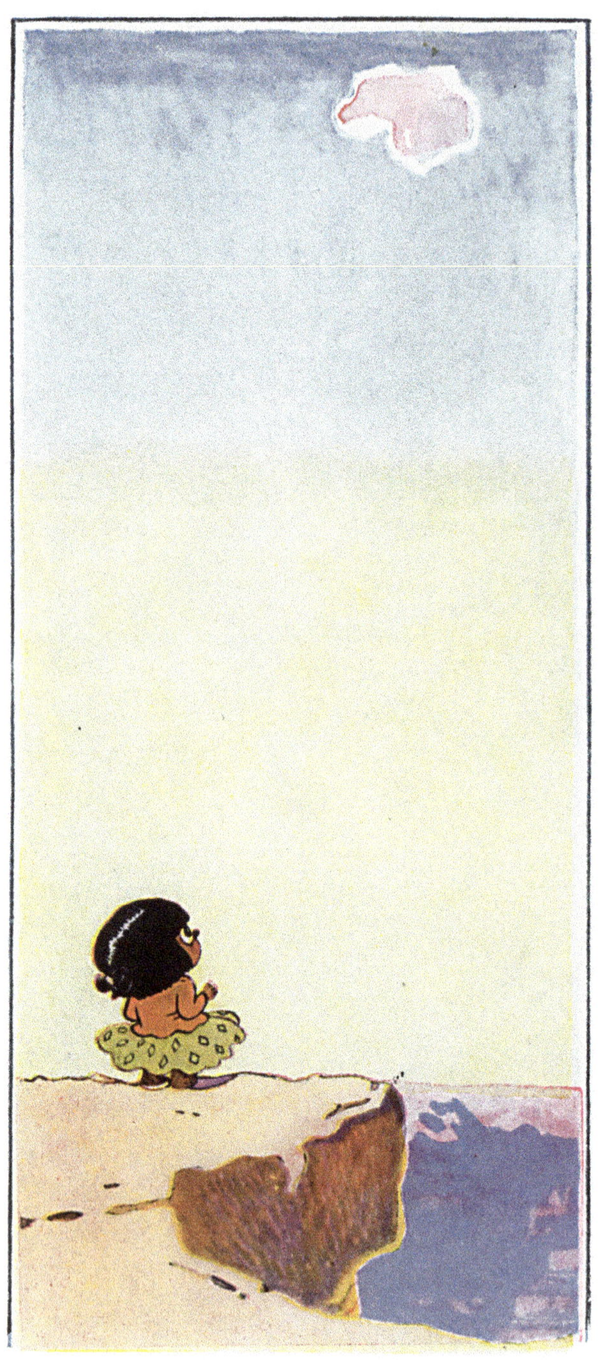

Little lonely cloud, up in the sky,
I know what I'd like to do
If I could find a way, I'd fly
'Way up and be company for you.

Little Ha-neck-ee had found
His daddy's peace pipe on the
ground.
He took a puff
One was enough
Now things are goin' 'round an'
'round.

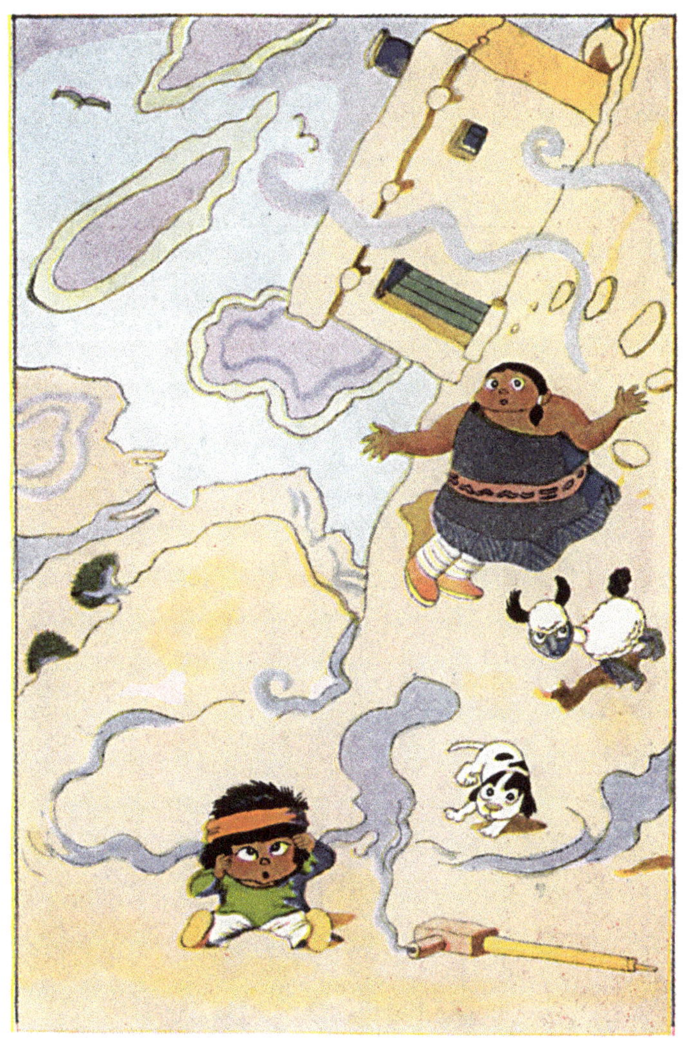

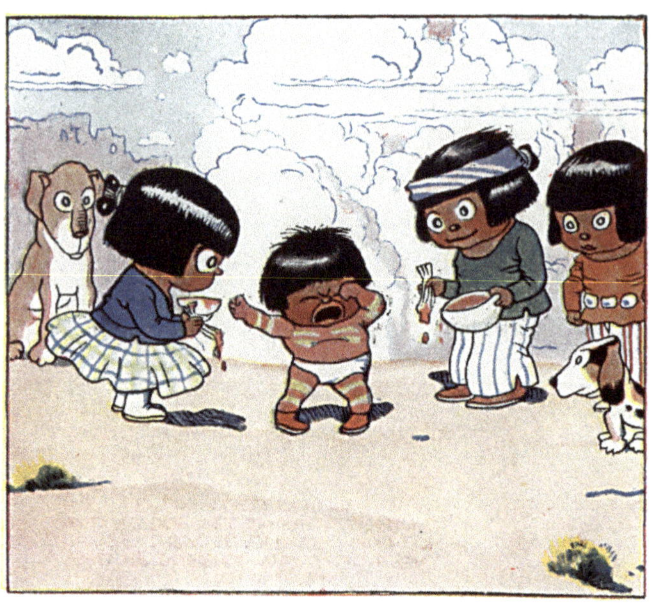

They've painted little Ho-tee-wa,
And he doesn't think it's right
'Cause they've painted him for war
And he doesn't want to fight.

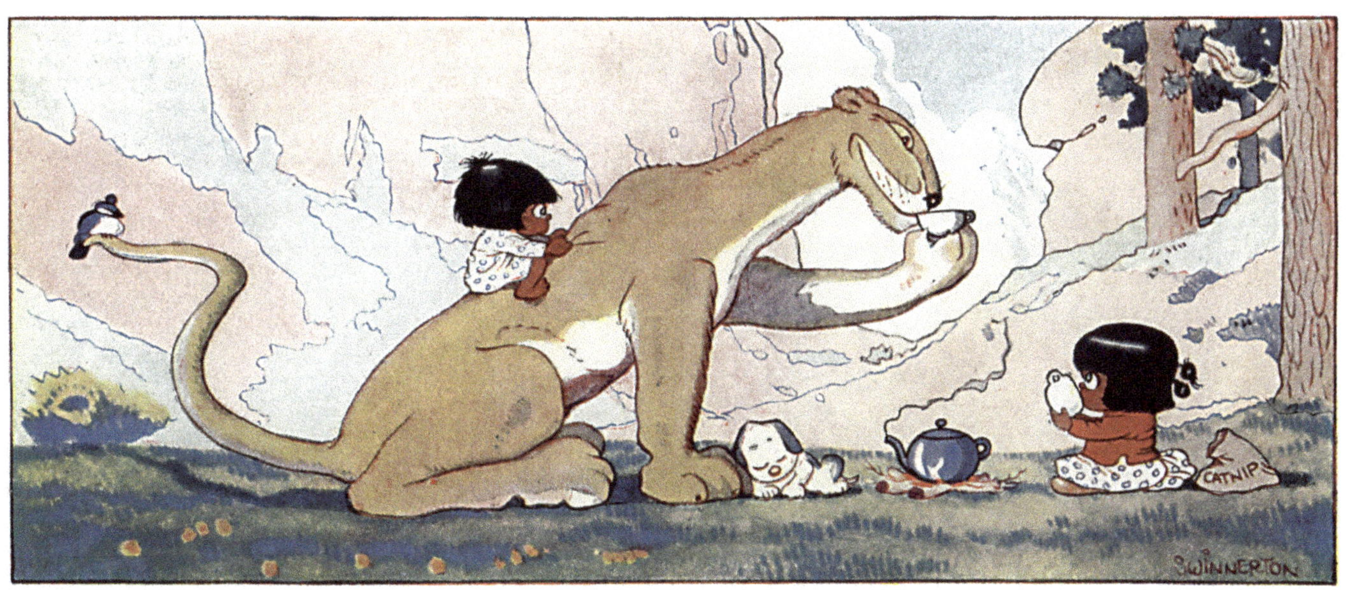

The big Mountain Lion is exceedingly tryin',
In that he'd very much like to eat you or me,
But he'll behave very fine, his politeness will shine
If you'll slip some catnip in his afternoon tea.

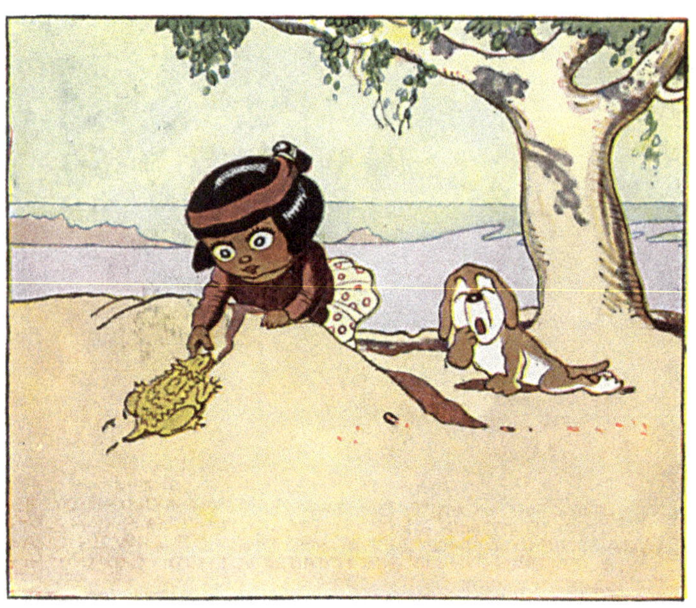

If you find a Horn-ed Toad a-sittin' in the sand,
You may play that you are putting him to bed.
And he will go right off to the Toad Slumber Land
If you only gently scratch him on his head.

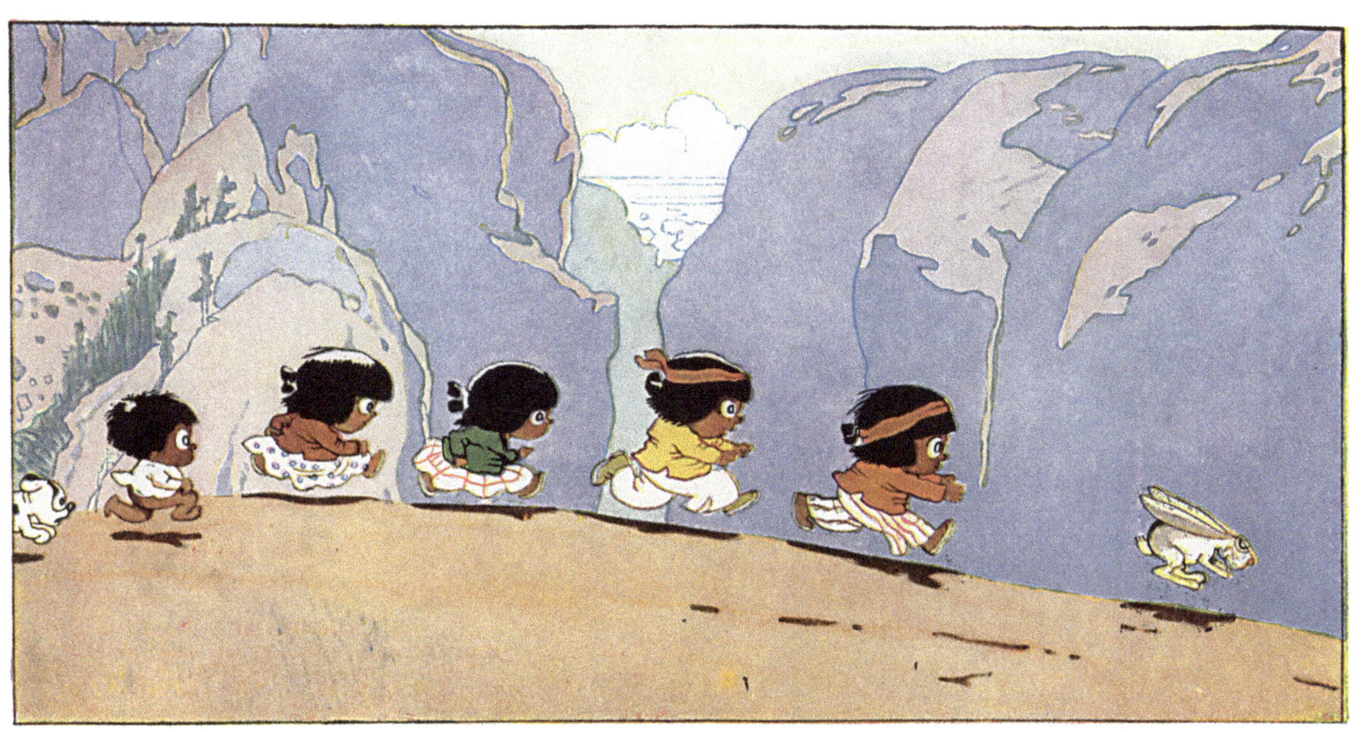

The Kiddies are chasing the Rabbit,
He's really quite safe, never fear;
Being chased is with him a habit,
He can keep safe in front for a year.

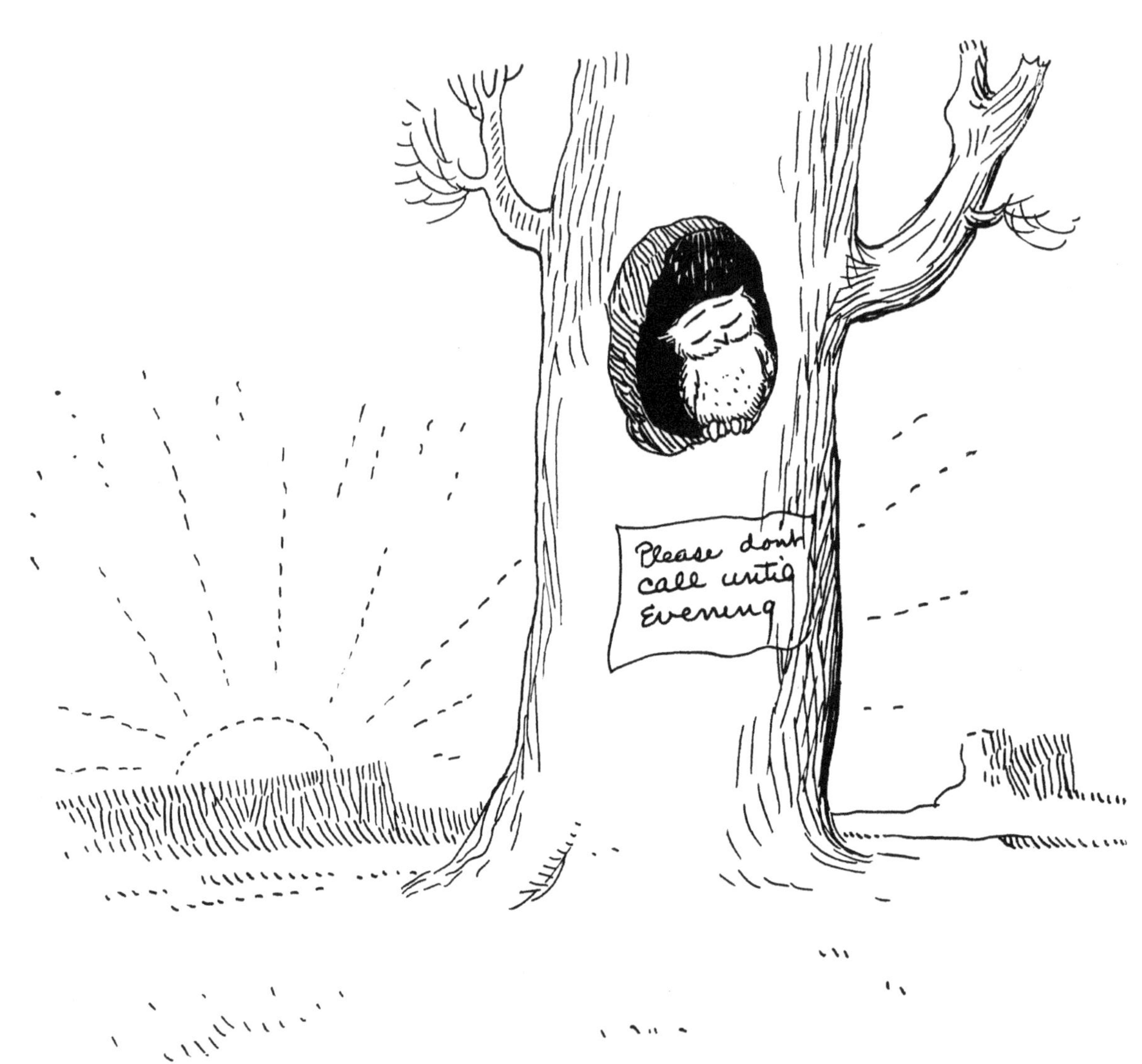
Please don't
call until
Evening

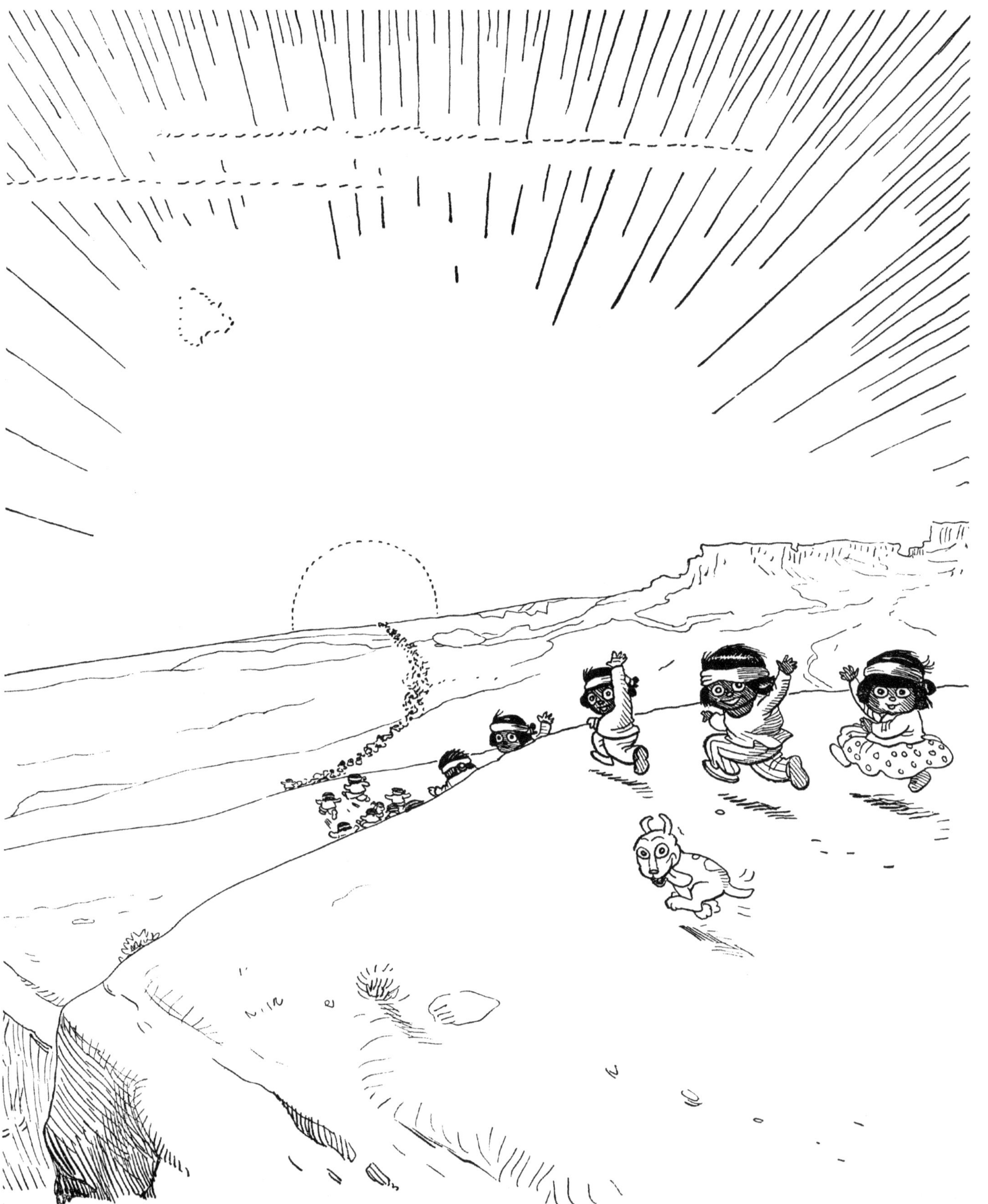

Coachwhip Publications

CoachwhipBooks.com

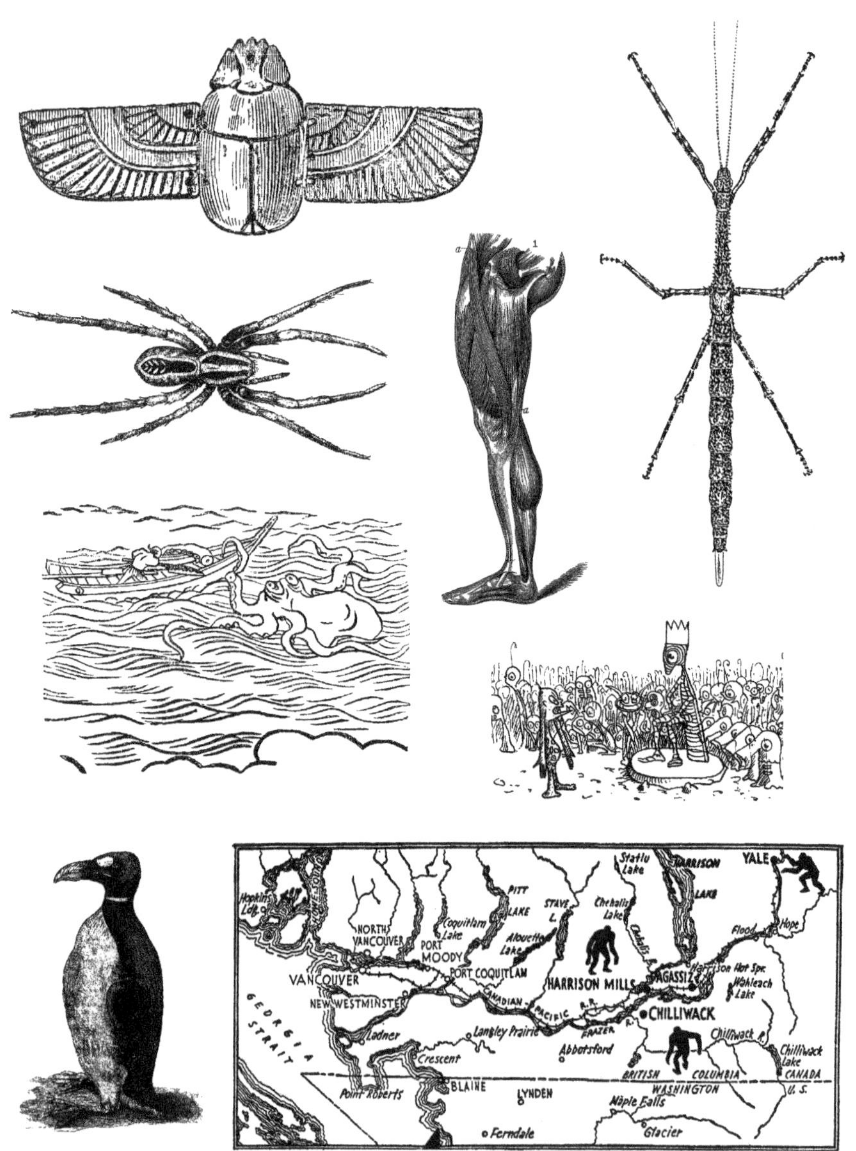

Coachwhip Publications

Also Available

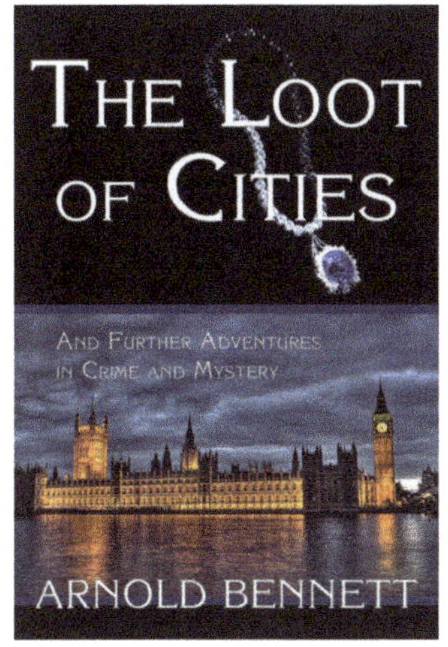

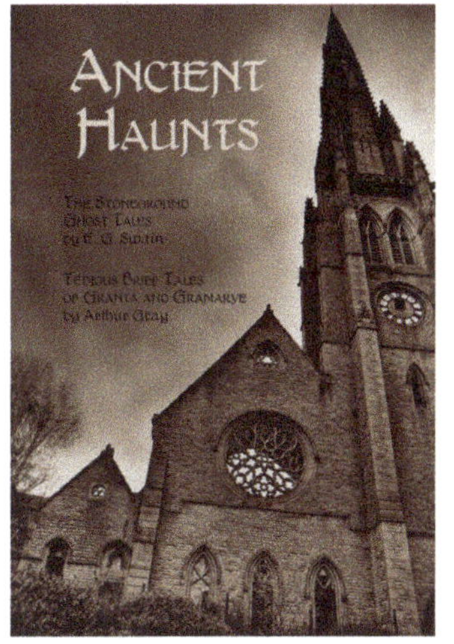

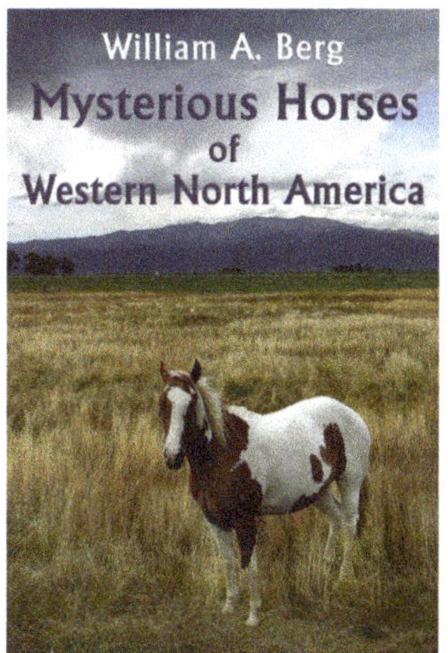

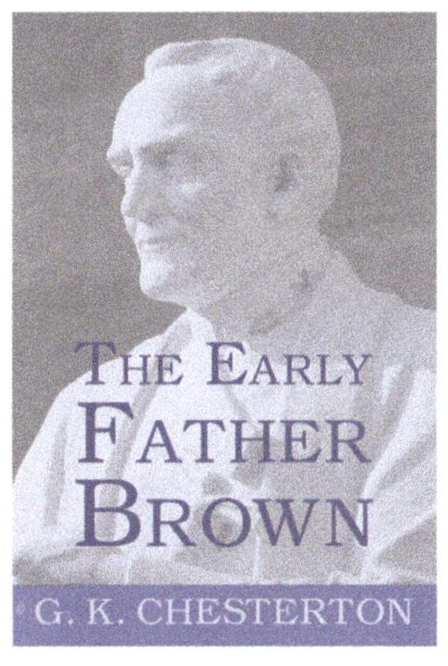

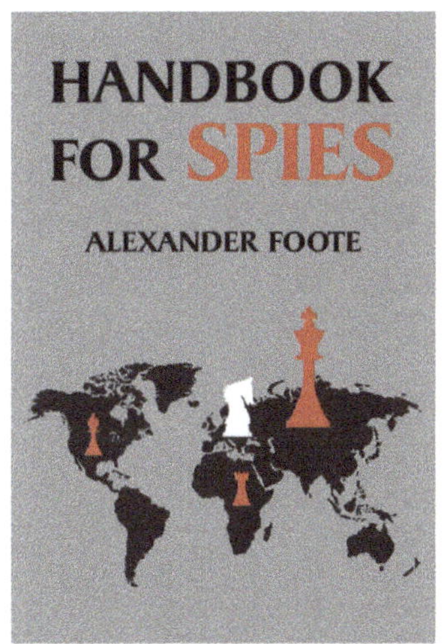

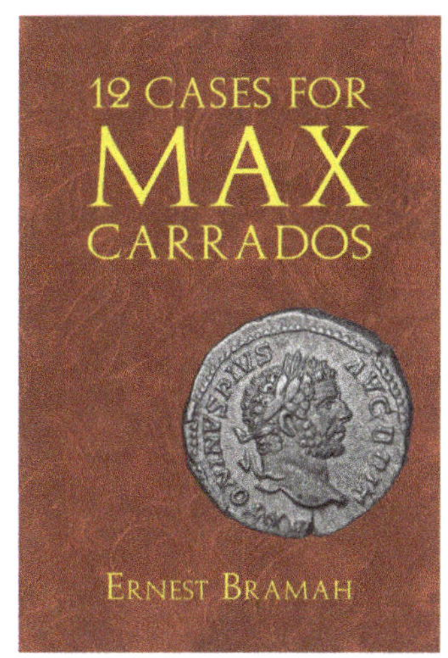

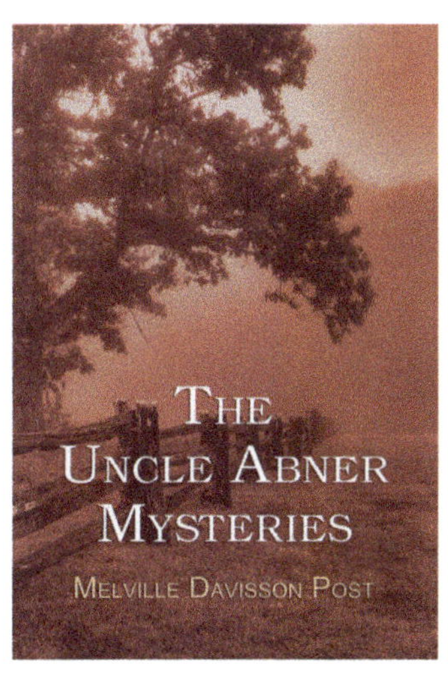

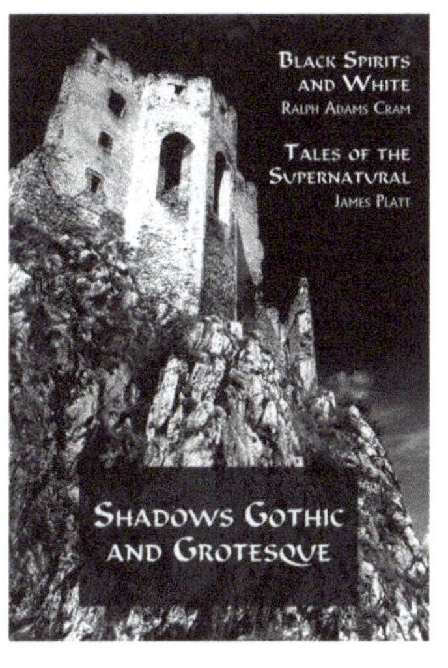

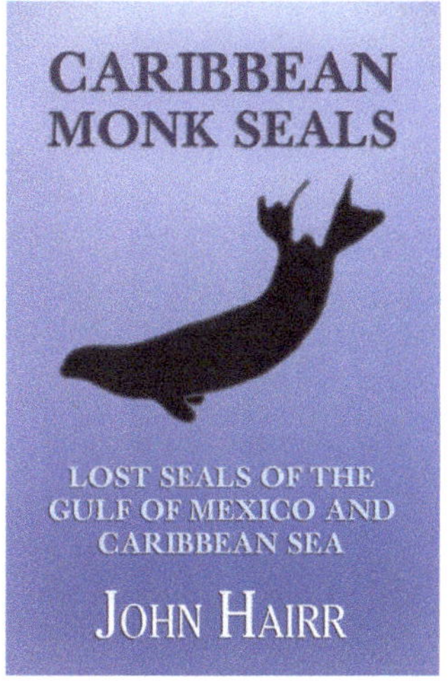

www.ingramcontent.com/pod-product-compliance
Lightning Source LLC
LaVergne TN
LVHW060632110826
845147LV00014B/898
* 9 7 8 1 6 1 6 4 6 0 7 0 9 *